SALVATION
AND BEHAVIOR

Romans 1-8, 12-15

SALVATION AND BEHAVIOR

Romans 1-8, 12-15

by

W. Graham Scroggie

KREGEL PUBLICATIONS
Grand Rapids, MI 49501

Salvation and Behavior by W. Graham Scroggie.
Published by Kregel Publications
a division of Kregel, Inc. All rights reserved.

Library of Congress Cataloging in Publication Data

Scroggie, William Graham, 1877-1958.
  Salvation and Behavior.

  Reprint of the 1952 ed. published by Pickering &
Inglis, London.
    1. Bible N.T. Romans — Criticism, interpretation, etc.
— Addresses, essays, lectures. I. Title.
BS2665.2.S38   1981   227'.106   80-8075
ISBN 0-8254-3735-0

Printed in the United States of America

CONTENTS

PHILOSOPHY OF SALVATION
(Romans 1:18-8:39)

1

THE CHRISTIAN MESSAGE
(Romans 1-5)

HAVING regard for the distinctiveness of this audience, and the design of this Convention, I have been led to call your attention this week to the subject of SALVATION and BEHAVIOUR as these are revealed and related in the Epistle to the Romans. They who would derive most profit from these studies should read each day chapters i-viii, and xii-xv; remembering, as you do so, that the first part treats of SALVATION, and the second, of BEHAVIOUR.

Between these two divisions of the Epistle is another —chapters ix-xi—integral to the whole, but as it is not essential for our present purpose we omit it.

This Epistle was written by Paul to the Church at Rome in A.D. 58. The occasion was the virtual close of his missionary ministry, and the object was to present in one comprehensive survey all that he had learned and taught, since his conversion, of the redeeming purpose and plan of God for mankind, as revealed in Jesus Christ.

The canonical and the chronological orders of Paul's Church Epistles are worthy of notice. 'Romans' was the sixth Letter to be written, but it is put first, because it is the foundation of all that follows; and the two Letters to Thessalonica, which were the first to be written, are placed at the end, because their subject is the Lord's Return, which is the last event.

'Romans' is the most systematic of all Paul's Epistles, and its importance cannot possibly be exaggerated. *Coleridge* called it 'the most profound writing extant.' *Godet* spoke of it as 'the greatest masterpiece which the human mind has ever conceived and realized; the first logical exposition of the work of God in Christ for the salvation of the world.' *Luther* described it as 'the chief part of the New Testament, and the perfect gospel.' *Calvin* said that 'every Christian man should feed upon it as the daily bread of his soul.' *Tholuck* called it 'a Christian philosophy of human history.' *Meyer* of Hanover described it as 'the greatest and richest of all the Apostolic works.' *Farrar* said, 'it is unquestionably the clearest and fullest statement of the doctrines of sin and deliverance from it, as held by the greatest of the Apostles.' *Chrysostom* used to have it read to him twice every week. And one more testimony: *William Tyndale* wrote, 'Forasmuch as this Epistle is . . . a light and way unto the whole Scripture, I think it meet that every Christian man not only know it by rote and without the book, but also exercise himself therein evermore continually, as with the daily bread of the soul. No man verily can read it too often, or study it too well; for the more it is studied, the easier it is; the more it is chewed, the pleasanter it is; and the more groundly it is searched, the preciouser things are found in it, so great treasure of spiritual things lieth hid therein.'

If this is what such men thought of the Epistle to the Romans, for any Christian not to have an intimate acquaintance with it, is something to be ashamed of, and to be remedied without delay. In this Epistle is a 'whole body of divinity,' and he who has a heart and mind possession of it is both Christian and cultured.

The *significance* of the Epistle is determined by its *scope*, and its scope is indicated by its *structure*. We must, therefore, discern its structure if we would appreciate and appropriate its profound truths. Between a Foreword (i. 1-17) and a Final Word (xv. 14-xvi. 27), there are three distinct divisions: chapters i-viii; ix-xi; and xii-xv. 13. The first is *Doctrinal*; the second is *Dispensational*; and the third is *Dutiful*.

The Epistle is the profoundest Christian philosophy; and the first division treats of the *Philosophy of Salvation*; the second, of the *Philosophy of History;* and the third, of the *Philosophy of Behaviour.*

That which gives unity to these three divisions is the subject of *God's Righteousness,* which is the keynote to the whole Epistle. It is introduced in ch. i. 16, 17:

> *I am not ashamed of the Gospel: it is the power of God*
> *for salvation to everyone who has faith, to the Jew first,*
> *and also to the Greek. For in it the righteousness of*
> *God is revealed through faith for faith; as it is written,*
> *"He who through faith is righteous shall live."*
> —(Revised Standard Version)

In chs. i-viii, *the Righteousness of God* is seen in relation to *Sins and Sin;* in chs. ix-xi, it is seen in relation to *the Calling of Israel;* and in chs. xii-xv. 13, it is seen in relation to *Everyday Life.* This outline should be rooted in the memory, and so be given a chance to bear fruit in the heart.

As has been said, we shall omit the second of these divisions, and so bring together the subjects of *Salvation* and *Behaviour.* To begin with, it is important to observe that in the New Testament Literature of the Church, creed and conduct are always related. *Doctrine and practice, theology and morality, knowledge and action* are inseparably connected, being related to one another as *foundation to superstructure,* as *centre to circumference,* as *root to fruit,* as *cause to effect.*

Some preachers expound without applying, and some endeavour to apply what has not been expounded, but the Apostles always do both. When revealed truth is divorced from Christian living it becomes an impotent abstraction. But Paul will have none of it. For him salvation must express itself in behaviour, and behaviour must embody salvation; and it is this which we are now to consider.

In the doctrinal division, chs. i. 18-viii. 39, the Apostle deals in detail with two things; the *Christian Message,* in chs. i. 18-v. 21, and the *Christian Life,* in chs. vi-viii, and it is made quite clear that there can be no such *Life* where there is no such *Message.*

When the Christian Message is not known or understood, the exhortation or effort to live the Christian Life is fatuous; it is as foolish as commencing to build a house from the roof. The Christian Message is an *origin,* and the Christian Life is an *issue.* The Christian Message tells of *Christ for us*; and the Christian Life relates to *Christ in us*; the one unfolds the *need* of redemption, and the other, the *way* of it; and these ideas cannot be transposed. If you would live a Christian life you must know what the Christian message is. When Dr. Dale first went to Birmingham, on his way home after a service one Sunday morning he met a brother minister who asked him what he had been preaching about. Dr. Dale told him that he had commenced a series on Christian doctrine; whereupon the other minister said: 'they won't stand doctrine in that church'; to which Dr. Dale replied, 'they'll have to'; and they did.

The only message to man which has substance and permanence is that which is expository, which is an unfolding of God's redeeming purpose and method. One may preach philosophy, or psychology, or ethics all his life, and yet accomplish nothing of permanent value, because those things are on the circumference of truth, and not at its centre.

What, then, is the content of the Christian Message in the view of Paul, the greatest of all theologians? He says that it has two dominating notes: CONDEMNATION, and JUSTIFICATION, and the message must be proclaimed in that order.

CONDEMNATION Romans 1:18-3:20

Like a wise master-builder, Paul begins with the foundation, and the foundation not *of*, but *for* the Christian message is the solemn, age-long and universal fact that all men are sinners, and so are under condemnation. Before considering what Paul has to say about Justification, it is necessary to contemplate what he says about man's state by nature, which makes Justification necessary. If man is not a sinner there is no need for Justification. The grace of God has for its background the guilt of man.

In dealing with this sombre subject the Apostle does not summarily state this fact, but so elaborates it that no possible doubt of it can remain. He does this in a thorough-going fashion; showing first, that *all Gentiles are under Condemnation;* then, that this is true of *all Jews* also; and so, finally, that *the whole world* is in a state of sin, and is guilty before God.

This solemn indictment, surely the most dreadful ever made, emerges from the revelation of the Gospel in ch. i. 16, 17, already quoted. Here eight great facts are affirmed of the Gospel. (1) As to *its nature,* it is 'Good News'; (2) as to *its source,* it is 'of God'; (3) as to *its greatness,* it is a revelation of God; (4) as to *its design,* its intention is salvation; (5) as to *its scope,* it is for 'everyone'; (6) as to *its efficiency,* it is God's power; (7) as to *its claim,* it must be 'believed'; and (8) as to *its outcome,* it issues in life. Of this Gospel Paul says he is 'not ashamed.' And why should he be? It tells of One, says Chrysostom, Who 'passed for the son of a carpenter, was brought up in Judæa in the home of a poor woman, and Who died like a criminal in the company of robbers.' Such a message was and is to Jews a stumblingblock, and to Gentiles, foolishness, but Paul was 'not ashamed' of it, for he judged it, not by its features, but by its fruits. There was a glory in the shame of Calvary, and a triumph in the seeming defeat.

On intellectual, social, and moral grounds, sinners object to the view that the Cross is a Gospel, but the intellectual, aristocratic, and ethical Paul proclaimed it to be such, and did so without fear or shame, as we shall see in this Letter.

Mankind is viewed in the light of this revelation; and first of all

1. The Gentiles are Indicted (1:18-32)

The Apostle makes clear three things: their *responsibility,* their *guilt,* and their *punishment.*

The RESPONSIBILITY of the Gentiles

Human responsibility is the cause of guilt, and punishment is the effect of it. Where there is no responsibility there can be no guilt, and where there is no guilt there can be no punishment; but THE GENTILES ARE RESPONSIBLE TO GOD, because He has revealed Himself to all such in the creation without, and to their conscience within.

Mark these two things carefully, *creation* and *conscience*. Because man is a rational and a moral being he has responsibility; that is, he has ability to respond to the manifestation of God in creation, and to the voice of God in his own conscience. This is true of all men, whether or not the Gospel ever reaches them. Man's *reason* reflecting on creation should lead him to recognize the power and perfections of God; and man's *conscience*, which is the faculty whereby he can distinguish between what is right and what is wrong, should lead him to approve the right and reject the wrong; and because heathenism has done neither of these things men have no excuse to offer God for their attitude towards Him.

Responsibility neglected leads to

The GUILT of the Gentiles

Because they have been negligent of the revelation which they have THEY ARE GUILTY BEFORE GOD; guilty of *perverseness* (18), of *irreligion* (21a), of *pride* (21b, 22), of *idolatry* (23, 25), of *sensuality* (24, 26, 27), of *wrongness* (28-31), and of *incorrigibility* (32).

The moral condition of the pagan world of the first century, which is vouched for by heathen writers such as Juvenal, Tacitus, and Petronius, is summarized by

ROMANS 1-5

Paul in twenty-one words of devastating description. The Gentiles were characterized by *iniquity, mischief, selfish greed, malice, envy, murder, quarrelsomeness, treachery,* and *malignity;* they were *whisperers, defamers, hateful to God, insolent, haughty, braggarts, inventors of evil, disobedient to parents, senseless, faithless, loveless,* and *pitiless.*

> On that hard Pagan world disgust
>   And secret loathing fell:
> Deep weariness and sated lust
>   Made human life a hell.
> In his cool hall with haggard eyes
>   The Roman noble lay;
> He drove abroad in furious guise
>   Along the Appian way;
> He made a feast, drank fierce and fast,
>   And crowned his hair with flowers—
> No easier nor no quicker passed
>   The impracticable hours.

Truly 'the heart is deceitful above all things, and desperately wicked'! Multitudes of Gentiles are not chargeable with many of these particular offences, but we all have that state of heart which produces them, though many people are refined by circumstances and culture. It is true of us all that we are guilty, because we are responsible.

The PUNISHMENT of the Gentiles

From these two facts emerges a third, which is inevitable and inexorable, and this is *punishment.* Guilt is the middle term between *responsibility* and *punishment,* and these stand in a morally organic relation to one another. *Responsibility* makes *guilt* possible, and these two make *punishment* certain.

Two things which these verses throw into prominence are the *attitude* and the *action* of God in relation to human guilt. His *attitude* is expressed in verse 18 as '*wrath*'; that is, His inherent antagonism to everything that is evil; and His *action*, expressive of His attitude, is stated in the thrice-repeated '*God gave them up*' (24, 26, 28); that is, He actively placed Himself against all sin by letting it work its inevitable ruin in the unrepentant sinner. The Divine verdict on incorrigible sinners is that they 'deserve to die' (32), and that death is at once their wages (vi. 23) and their sentence. There is no escape from the guilt, the pollution, the power, and the final consequences of sin and sins except under cover of Christ's 'precious blood.'

There is no doubt, then, about the guilt of the Gentiles, and with this verdict the Jews are in entire agreement. But the Apostle now turns his attention to them, and in what follows

2. THE JEWS ARE INDICTED (2:1-3:8)

'You have no excuse, O man, whoever you are, when you judge another; for in passing judgment upon him you condemn yourself, because you, the judge, are doing the very same things. Do you suppose, O man, that when you judge those who do such things and yet do them yourself, that you will escape the judgment of God?' (ii. 1, 3).

In this long section, which throughout has the Jews chiefly in view, four principles of Divine judgment are affirmed.

Firstly, GOD'S JUDGMENT IS TRUE (2:2)
'*The judgment of God is according to truth.*'
The judgment of the Jew was false, because he

thought that God would spare the descendants of Abraham as such, on account of their national and religious privileges. But these very privileges made the guilt of the Jew more evident, and his accountability more certain (2-5).

Secondly, GOD's JUDGMENT IS JUST (6)

He *'will render to every man according to his deeds.'*

The standard of God's decision is moral action and its opposite. The character of each of us as God sees us, Jew or Gentile, is the criterion whereby God regards us (6-10).

Thirdly, GOD's JUDGMENT IS IMPARTIAL (11)

'For there is no respect of persons with Him.'

Jews have the Mosaic Law and their conscience; Gentiles have their conscience, but not the Mosaic Law; and each will be judged by what he has, not by what he has not. The primacy and priority of the Jew does not make his sin less sinful, but rather deepens his guilt because his light is greater; and the fact that the Gentile did not receive the Mosaic Law does not make his sin more sinful, but he will be judged by his moral condition, for the Divine judgment is without partiality (11-15).

Fourthly, GOD's JUDGMENT IS ACCORDING TO THE REDEEMING CHRIST (16)

He *'will judge the secrets of men by Jesus Christ according to my Gospel.'*

Every man, Jew and Gentile, is and will at last be confronted with Jesus Christ Who is the manifestation of God's redeeming purpose, and it is a man's attitude towards Him that is determinative.

But the Jews raise objections to all this, and want to know of what value Judaism is, if Jews are placed spiritually on a level with Gentiles. The Apostle answers these objections (iii. 1-8), and summarizes all that he has already said, in the statement:

'*We have before proved both Jews and Gentiles, that they are all under sin*' (iii. 9). And so

3. THE WHOLE WORLD IS INDICTED (3:9-20)

In a number of quotations from the Scriptures of the Jews Paul proves that all men are under sin; a fact which is made evident in man's character (10-12) and conduct (13-17); and the cause of this is practical irreligion; 'there is no fear of God before their eyes' (18). No one, therefore, can claim to be righteous, for 'all the world has come under judgment in respect of God' (iii. 19).

God's description of man's fallen state is a terrible one. Here are fourteen affirmations—twice the number of completeness—

> There is none righteous, no, not one;
> There is none that understandeth,
> There is none that seeketh after God;
> They have all turned aside,
> They are together become unprofitable;
> There is none that doeth good, no, not so much
>   as one;
> Their throat is an open sepulchre;
> With their tongues they have used deceit;
> The poison of asps is under their lips;
> Whose mouth is full of cursing and bitterness;
> Their feet are swift to shed blood;
> Destruction and misery are in their ways;
> And the way of peace have they not known;
> There is no fear of God before their eyes.

ROMANS 1-5

This is not a message which people want to hear, and it is not one which preachers wish to deliver; but wrong diagnosis at the beginning must lead to wrong treatment of man's need, which, alas, too often is the case. The fact of total depravity lies in the foundation of the Christian Message, for the News which is Good implies the state which is bad. The uncondemned do not need a reprieve; the healthy do not need a physician; and the righteous do not need a Saviour. Supply presupposes want, and salvation implies sinfulness. The pride of man rebels against the truth about himself, but in so doing he is despising the grace of God, and is incurring the Divine wrath.

As John the Baptist with his message of 'wrath to come' preceded Jesus with His message of 'come unto Me,' so, in Romans, the affirmation of Condemnation precedes the exposition of Justification.

In this Epistle the 'love' of God is referred to six times, and the 'wrath' of God, ten times; but His 'wrath' is an aspect of His 'love.' Why is a mother angry with her child for playing with fire? Because she loves her. The 'wrath' of God is not a passion, but a principle, and for this reason prominence is given to it in this Compendium of Christian Truth.

But the proof of human depravity in chs. i. 18-iii. 20 is not the Gospel; it but makes evident the need for it. If one preached nothing but condemnation for fifty years, he would not once have preached the Gospel. To declare that a man is sick is not to cure him. Let the young evangelist and preacher remember this; and may the 'liberal' preacher, so-called, learn that salvation is not from within outward, but from without inward, for we can 'work out' only what God 'works in' (Phil. ii. 12, 13).

So now we come to the second part of the Christian Message, which, in the light of what has been said, is in fact that Message.

JUSTIFICATION Romans 3:21-5:11

This word, with its equivalents, is one of the key-words of the Epistle, occurring about fifty times; and these chapters, iii-v, are the greatest on the subject in the New Testament. The experience of which this word speaks is not easy to expound. The meaning is, *to pronounce righteous,* NOT *to make righteous,* for what is *imputed* is not in fact *imparted*; but *to be justified means that,* in the way here indicated, *the believer is viewed in Christ as righteous, and is treated as such by God.*

Whatever may be its exact theological meaning, we may confidently say that *justification is the opposite of condemnation*; the one is man's state *in Christ,* as the other is his state *out of Christ,* and no one can be in both states at the same time. Condemnation is universal, but justification is not, because while all are *fallen,* not all are *forgiven.*

Let us see, then, what the Apostle has to say about this wonderful thing called Justification. His thought is as clear and precise here as we have seen it to be in the previous section, and he introduces the subject by using two words to indicate the change of theme. He says 'BUT NOW'; a term which may be regarded as *logical,* contrasting the states of condemnation and justification; and as *temporal,* contrasting the past with the present. Paul seems to give a sigh of relief when he reaches this point and says, '*but now.*' It occurs in

ROMANS 1-5

a like connection in Eph. ii. 12, 13, where the Apostle, after having said of believing Gentiles that 'in time past' they had been without Christ—aliens—and strangers, 'having no hope, and without God in the world,' he hastens to say, '*but now*, in Christ Jesus, ye who once were far off, are made nigh by the blood of Christ.'

'*But*' refers to the *past*, and '*now*,' to the *present*. After *ruin* comes *redemption*; and after *penury* comes *provision*.

What, then, are the dominating notes of the new theme? There are three: the *Ground*, the *Means*, and the *Effect* of Justification. The Ground of it is *God's Grace*; the Means of it is *our Faith*; and the Effect of it is *Assurance*.

Firstly, then,

THE GROUND OF JUSTIFICATION IS GOD'S GRACE
(3:21-26)

'Justified freely by His grace, through the redemption that is in Christ Jesus' (24).

This passage may be regarded as the very heart of the whole Epistle, because the heart of the Gospel is Calvary. In the Old Testament everything leads up to the Cross, and in the New Testament everything flows from it, and so, in this Classic of the Christian Life, the Apostle shows *first* of all the need of fallen man for the intervention of God; and *finally*, the outcome in Christian character and conduct of that intervention; and *centrally*, between these two, the nature of the intervention is revealed in the death of Christ as an atoning Sacrifice.

This paragraph (21-26) is amazing for its fulness of thought. The 'righteousness' referred to has its *source* in God, it is *His* righteousness; it is *'manifested,'* that is, *revealed,* for man could not have discovered it; it is *independent,* 'apart from the Law,' for man could not merit it; it was *predicted,* for it is 'according to the law and the prophets'; it is *bestowed,* for we are 'justified freely by His grace'; as a gift it is *costly,* because it is 'through the redemption' of Christ on Calvary; it is *atoning,* because Christ's shed blood was a 'propitiation'; it is *ethical,* for God's 'forbearance' with the sins of mankind for millenniums was not due to indifference, but He 'passed them over' because He was on His way to Calvary; and it is *effective* and *final,* for it is the 'just' God who 'justifies' men; that is, God is just in justifying.

All this is wonderful, most wonderful! Come, ye rebellious and unbelieving; listen, ye depressed and despairing; look, ye faltering and failing; meet Christ at Calvary; God our Maker is our Redeemer; He against Whom we have sinned is offering us salvation.

> Grace! 'tis a charming sound,
>   Harmonious to the ear;
> Heaven with its echo shall resound,
>   And all the earth shall hear.

> Grace all the work shall crown
>   Through everlasting days:
> It lays in heaven the topmost stone,
>   And well deserves the praise.

It was in an hour of despair that William Cowper read this passage, and he says:

'On reading it I immediately received power to believe. The rays of the Sun of Righteousness fell on me in all their fulness; I saw the complete sufficiency of the expiation which Christ had wrought for my pardon and entire justification. In an instant I believed, and received the peace of the Gospel. . . . My eyes filled with tears; transports choked my utterance. I could only look to heaven in silent fear, overflowing with love and wonder.'

'The grace of God that bringeth salvation hath appeared unto all men' (Tit. ii. 11).

'We beseech you that ye receive not the grace of God in vain' (2 Cor. vi. 1).

This leads us to the second note in this portion of the Message, namely, that

THE MEANS OF JUSTIFICATION IS OUR FAITH
(3:27-4:25)

Faith is another of the keywords of 'Romans', and references to it, or the want of it, occur sixty-four times in the Epistle. This quality is more easily described than defined, but we can definitely exclude *credulity* and *presumption* from the idea. Faith, in an evangelical context, is confidence in God and His Word. It is an assurance that what He has promised to do He will do. It is reliance upon God's known character. It is the re-echo in man's consciousness of the Divine Voice.

It may be said that in saving faith there are three elements. The first relates to the *intellect*, which accepts the evangelical facts, and the interpretation of them as given in the Records. But this alone

cannot save.   The second element relates to *feeling*.
The convicted sinner recognizes that God's provision
in Christ for him is the answer to his need.   But even
knowledge and *emotion* together cannot bring one into
salvation.   One thing more is needed, and this is
found in *an act of the will*.   The sinner conscious of his
need, and beholding the provision, believes Christ
to be wholly trustworthy, and takes Him to be his
personal Saviour.

ROMANS 1-5

Faith in this sense is the universal condition of
salvation, and is intensely personal; and it is the
germinal grace of the Christian life.   There is no
saving virtue in faith, and yet, without faith we cannot
be saved.   Righteousness is not *attained* by *works*, but
it is *obtained* by *faith*.   As the virtue of a banknote is
not in itself, but in the bank, so the virtue of faith is
not in itself, but in its Object.   Trust is man's answer
to God's truth.   Though the word *alone* does not
occur in the text, Luther's dictum, 'justification by
faith in Christ *alone*' is correct, because justification
is not by works at all.

In expounding this truth Paul shows that justification
by faith, not by law-keeping, is the teaching of the Old
Testament, for Abraham was justified by faith centuries before the Mosaic Law was given (ch. iv.).

> 'If Abraham were justified by works, he hath
> whereof to glory; but not before God' (iv. 2).

God *credited* the Patriarch with faith, not with works;
and so it says:

> 'Abraham *believed* God, and it was *counted* unto him
> for righteousness' (iv. 3, 9).

And long after the Law was given, David describes

'the blessedness of the man unto whom God *imputes* righteousness apart from works' (iv. 6).

The fact is, therefore, that the blessing of justification must be *accepted by faith* by Jew and Gentile alike. Of this initial and supreme blessing God's grace is the *source*; Christ's blood is the *power*; man's faith is the *instrument*; Christ's resurrection is the *assurance*; and 'good works' are the *evidence*.

And now we come to the third note in the truth about Justification. We have seen that it originates in the grace of God, and that it is apprehended and appropriated by faith; but the question may well be asked, 'Is this not too good to be true?'; to which the Apostle replies: 'No, not too good to be true, but true because it is so good'. And so, thirdly,

THE EFFECT OF JUSTIFICATION IS ASSURANCE
(5:1-11)

This assurance is rooted in the fact that the blessing of Justification is '*through our Lord Jesus Christ*,' a phrase with which the passage begins and ends (1, 11); and what is 'through' Him is thorough.

The assurance which this passage embodies covers the whole life of the justified man, past, present, and future, so that the blessing which has begun will continue, and will be consummated at last. The passage begins with '*therefore*,' the first of three occurrences in the Epistle which gather up the preceding argument and carry the exposition forward.

The first is the '*therefore*' *of justification* (v. 1), and relates to the section iii. 21-iv. 25;

'*Therefore* being justified by faith,'

The second is the *'therefore' of sanctification* (viii. 1),
and relates to the section vi-vii:

> 'There is *therefore* now no condemnation to them
> that are in Christ Jesus . . . who walk not after the
> flesh, but after the Spirit' (viii. 1, 4).

The third is the *'therefore' of dedication* (xii. 1), and
relates to all that has gone before (i.-xi):

> 'I beseech you *therefore*, brethren, to present your
> bodies a living sacrifice.'

The first relates to the *soul*; the second, to the
spirit; and the third, to the *body*; and thus our attention
is drawn to *salvation, sanctification,* and *service.* The
first introduces us to *Christian assurance*; the second, to
Christian attainment; and the third, to *Christian activity.*
Let us look now at the first of these.

(i) *Assurance as to the Past* (v. 1)

The Apostle says 'Having-been-justified by faith.'
The theology of this is in the tense. It is the *aorist,*
which means that our justification is already accomplished; and it is the *passive participle,* which means
that it is God who has justified us, and not we ourselves; and it is reaffirmed that by faith we were put
in touch with this blessing.

There is a truth which we should continuously
contemplate: 'we have been, and now are, justified.'
One commentator says that this, and such passages,
'do not warrant the doctrine of assurance, in the sense
that an individual believer may and ought to feel
certain of his own final salvation on the ground of
having once been justified.'

That statement is a denial of one of the fundamental truths of the Christian Faith, and strikes at the very heart of the Gospel. We who have been justified by God are justified for ever.

(ii) *Assurance as to the Present* (1, 2)

Two things are here affirmed: first, that 'we have peace with God,' and secondly, that 'we have had (and now have) access into (Divine) grace.' Here is amazing wealth of truth for our present assurance.

'*Peace with God*' means that the war between us and God is at an end. Peace has been made by the blood of the Cross, and God now looks, not at our sins, but at Christ's blood. 'He is our peace,' not because of what He is now doing in heaven, but because of what long ago He did on Calvary. One cannot have 'the peace of God' without having 'peace with God,' but one may have the latter without the former.

> I hear the words of love,
> I gaze upon the blood,
> I see the mighty Sacrifice,
> And *I have peace with God.*

Then, it is said that 'we have access into this grace wherein we stand.'

'*Access into grace*' here, means that we have been *introduced* into the sphere of justification of which Paul has been speaking, and there we abide; and it is in this atmosphere that we 'have peace with God.' In these immortal words we who are justified are assured of *peace* and *acceptance*, and of peace because of acceptance.

And now, in the third place, we are vouchsafed

(iii) *Assurance as to the Future* (2)

'We rejoice in hope of the glory of God.'

'*The Glory of God*' means the Glory of His Presence, His brightness and splendour, which was symbolized by the Shekinah over the Mercy Seat in the Tabernacle of old. The Apostle says that participation in this Glory is the believer's 'hope.' Not only at last shall we enter into that Glory, but we shall also partake of it; we shall be 'glorified with Him' (viii. 17). Because of this we are to 'exult', vocally to 'boast'. This is a consequence of our justification which lies in the eternal future, and in which we should now rejoice.

The Apostle goes on to say that afflictions cannot destroy this hope (3-5); that it is confirmed by God's great love manifested in Christ (6-8); and so we may make our boast in God Who, through Christ, has vouchsafed to us this reconciliation.

SUMMARY (5:12-21)

CONDEMNATION AND JUSTIFICATION TRACED TO THEIR HISTORICAL SOURCES IN ADAM AND CHRIST

Having expounded the momentous themes of *Condemnation* and *Justification,* Paul now traces these to their historical sources in Adam and Christ in ch. v. 12-21, before passing on to the subject of the Christian Life in chs. vi-viii.

Here is the great doctrine of *The Two Men, Adam* and *Christ. Condemnation* is traced to the one, and *Justification* to the other. By Adam's one sin *death came* to all mankind; and by Christ's one act on the Cross *life comes* to all who believe. Through Adam *sin abounds,* but through Christ *grace much more abounds,*

Through the first Adam has come *ruin*, and through the Last Adam has come *redemption*.

In this way the foundations are laid on which the rest of the Epistle is built. The *need* for the *Christian Message*, in man's *Condemnation*, and the *nature* of it, in Divine *Justification* (i-v), prepare the way for the *Christian Life* which is now to be expounded in its two aspects of *Sanctification* and *Glorification* (vii-viii).

> And can it be that I should gain
>   An interest in the Saviour's blood?
> Died He for me, who caused His pain?
>   For me, who Him to death pursued?
> Amazing love! how can it be
>   That Thou, my God, shouldst die for me?
>
> No condemnation now I dread;
>   Jesus, and all in Him, is mine!
> Alive in Him, my living Head,
>   And clothed in righteousness divine,
> Bold I approach the eternal throne,
>   And claim the crown, through Christ, my own.

'Thanks be unto God for His unspeakable Gift.'

2

THE CHRISTIAN LIFE
(Romans 6-8)

IN unfolding the *Philosophy of Salvation* (chs. i-viii), the Apostle discusses four great topics: *Condemnation; Justification; Sanctification;* and *Glorification;* topics which embrace the whole of the Christian Gospel.

These four subjects are divided into two and two: the first two, *Condemnation* and *Justification,* constitute *the Christian Message;* and the second two, *Sanctification* and *Glorification,* interpret *the Christian Life.*

The first two tell of *Christ's work for us*—the *need* of it, and the *nature* of it; and the second two tell of *Christ's work in us,* in the *present,* and in the *future.*

We have considered the first two of these subjects; and now we must contemplate the second two, which are a wonderful exposition of the Christian Life as it *should now be,* and *ultimately will be.* *Sanctification* tells of the *present process,* and *Glorification,* of the *final issue.*

SANCTIFICATION Romans 6:1-8:17

This statement in chs. vi-viii is the classic on the subject of the Christian Life, and cannot be given too close attention. Parts of it have frequently been treated at this Convention, but I am not aware that at any time the whole of it has been considered in its relation to the entire Epistle; yet such a view is of the utmost importance. The first five chapters are the *foundation* on which the *superstructure* of chapters six to eight rests. Not only must the *Christian Message* be believed before the *Christian Life* can be lived, but the *Christian Life* is the proof that the *Christian Message* has been believed. There cannot be fruit where there is no root, but the proof of the root is the fruit.

Our Justification is in the Crucified Saviour, and our Sanctification is in the Risen Lord. By the separation of these two subjects in the Church's thinking and teaching, the loss in Christian experience has been incalculable. Justification by faith in Christ is only the beginning of God's purpose for us, and the continuance of that purpose is a life lived according to a revealed pattern. What that pattern is, appears in chapters vi-viii of this Epistle.

There are over 650 references to holiness in the Bible, and while the word is not easy to define, its meaning is not obscure. Sanctification is not sanctimoniousness, but it *is* sanctity, which is holiness of life, and what is meant by holiness of life these three chapters reveal. Let us, first of all, glance at them as a whole. The three chapters may be divided into two parts. Part 1 is *Mystical* (vi. 1-vii. 6), and Part 2 is *Experimental* (vii. 7-viii. 17). The *Mystical* part treats of profound spiritual truths which can be apprehended only by faith. The *Experimental* part is autobiographical, and therein the Apostle tells us what his own experience has been.

In what is a very comprehensive statement, four things are impressed upon our attention.

In the first place, the *Principle of Holiness* is stated, which consists in the individual's identification with Christ in His death and resurrection (vi. 1-11). This leads to a consideration of the *Practice of Holiness,* which is realized in the believer's abandonment to his new relations as a Christian (vi. 12-vii. 6).

But such a life will not go unchallenged, and so the *Preventive of Holiness* is set forth, which is seen to be the activity within of sin and of self (vii. 7-25).

And finally, the *Power of Holiness* is shown to be the unhindered dominion over us of the Holy Spirit (viii. 1-17).

Here nothing is omitted which would help us better to understand and more fully to realize what Christ meant when He said: 'I am come that ye might have life (chs. i-v), and that ye might have it abundantly' (chs. vi-viii. 17).

THE PRINCIPLE OF HOLINESS (6:1-11)

The key to this profound portion of 'Romans' is found in two words in ver. 4, *'newness of life.'* The word for 'life' (zōē) does not refer to its manner, but to its principle; and the word 'newness' 'expresses not so much youth as *novelty,'* and it will be seen that the Apostle is speaking of *life that is quite new.*

To know what this life is will reveal to us the innermost meaning of sanctification.

The Apostle is not now dealing with justification and the removal of guilt, which has been discussed in chs. i-v, and is assumed; but he is dealing with that for which we were justified, a life rooted in a principle which, if apprehended and believed, is productive of holiness.

What, then, is this principle? It is the Christian's recognition of his *identification with Christ in His death and resurrection.* Paul, along with all believers of his

ROMANS 6-8

day, had been baptized, and he makes this symbolic witness the basis of his argument. He says, in effect:

> 'Surely you must recognize that your baptism symbolized your identification with Christ in three respects: with His *death*, His *burial*, and His *resurrection*. When you went down into the water, you admitted *death*; when you went under it, you admitted *burial*; and when you emerged from it, you admitted *resurrection*.'

'Baptism,' says Bishop Headlam, 'expresses symbolically a series of acts corresponding to the redeeming acts of Christ. Immersion symbolizes Death; Submersion symbolizes Burial; and Emergence symbolizes Resurrection.'

This symbolic practice is not a matter of denominational controversy, but of historical fact, and Paul would bring home to us all the significance of the fact.

> 'Do you not know that all of us who have been baptized into Christ Jesus were baptized into His death? We were buried therefore with Him by baptism into death, so that as Christ was raised from the dead by the glory of the Father, we too might walk in newness of life' (3, 4).

This identification with Christ is the profoundest truth in the New Testament, and is both an exposure of all false theories of holiness, and a challenge to the common experience of Christian people. We who in Adam were 'dead *in* sin,' are now in Christ 'dead *to* sin.'

What is here declared *is a fact for faith,* and *not an emotion for experience,* and it is squarely based on the immediately preceding passage concerning the federal headships of Adam and Christ (v. 12-21). Our state by nature is one of sin under the headship of Adam, and our state by grace is one of death to sin under the headship of Christ. The word 'such as we' (hŏtinĕs) at the beginning of verse two makes it plain that the Apostle is referring to Christians only, and to *all* Christians, and he says that '*such as we died to sin.*' This note dominates the passage and must be clearly understood.

And now a bit of grammar. In the Greek New Testament there is a tense which is peculiar to the language, and which has a most important significance wherever it occurs. It is the *aorist* tense, which denotes *a single and completed past act,* and thus it differs from the *imperfect* and *perfect* tenses. This tense occurs eleven times in these eleven verses, with reference to our identification with Christ in death, burial, and resurrection. Mark what the passage says:

Ver. 2. 'We *died* to sin.'
Ver. 3. 'We *were baptized* into His death' (twice).
Ver. 4. 'We *were buried* with Him into death.
Ver. 4. 'We *were raised up* from the dead.'
Ver. 6. 'Our old self *was crucified* with Him.'
Ver. 7. 'He who *died*', i.e. Christ.
Ver. 8. 'We *died* with Christ.'
Ver. 9. 'Christ *raised* from the dead.'
Ver. 10. 'He *died*' (twice), i.e. Christ.

These references mean that as definitely as Christ by an act died, and by an act was raised from the dead, so in His death and resurrection every believer died to sin and rose to 'newness of life.' Our 'old self was crucified' when Christ was crucified. All we were and are from Adam God has rejected, and *judicially,* not *experimentally,* it was put an end to. The crucifixion of self is not something that we can accomplish, for it was accomplished on Calvary. In chs. i-v we are shown that *Christ died for us,* and in ch. vi we are told that *we died with Him.*

Christ died both *for* sin and *unto* it. We could not die *for* it, but in Christ's death we did die *unto* it. Then and there He made His own relation to sin the believer's relation to it, so that we are to 'reckon ourselves dead to sin, and living to God.' In consequence Paul asks how we can continue to live in that to which we died (2). The reference is not to the committal of separate acts of sin, but to *the habit of sinning.* 'Whosoever is born of God does not practise—continue in a course of—sin; . . . he is not able to practise sin, because he is born of God' (1 John iii. 6, 9).

Well did Tersteegen write:

> Dead and crucified with Thee,
>   passed beyond my doom;
> Sin and law for ever silenced in the tomb.
> Passed beyond the mighty curse, dead,
>   from sin set free;
> Not for Thee earth's joy and music,
>   not for me.
> Dead, the sinner past and gone,
>   not the sin alone,
> Living, where Thou art in glory on the Throne.

We have given detailed attention to this *Principle of Holiness* because of its tremendous importance for an understanding of the innermost significance of being a Christian.

But just because this truth is not merely a theological and mystical theory, but something living and energetic Paul passes on to the consideration of

THE PRACTICE OF HOLINESS (6:12-7:6)

On the part of the Christian this consists in *the recognition of, and abandonment to the new relations* consequent upon our identification with Christ in His death and resurrection; and three aspects of these relations are given:

King and Subject (vi. 12-14); *Master and Servant* (vi. 15-23); and *Husband and Wife* (vii. 1-6).

First, then, is the illustration of

KING AND SUBJECT (6:12-14)

In order better to understand this paragraph, I will read to you the paraphrase of Sanday and Headlam.

> 'I exhort you therefore not to let Sin exercise its tyranny over this frail body of yours by giving way to its evil passions. Do not, as you are wont, place hand, eye, and tongue, as weapons stained with unrighteousness, at the service of sin; but dedicate yourselves once for all, like men who have left the ranks of the dead and breathe a new spiritual life, to God; let hand, eye, and tongue be weapons of righteous temper for Him to wield. You may rest assured that in so doing Sin will have no claim or power over you, for you have left the *régime* of Law for that of Grace.'

Clearly the metaphor here used is that of a *King and a Subject*. The paragraph begins with the word '*reign*,' and ends with the word '*dominion*.' Sin 'is conceived of as a *ruler* employing the members of man as weapons of warfare, wherewith to contend against the government of God, and to establish unrighteousness' (H. A. W. Meyer).

In the New Testament there is *a doctrine of the body,* and in this Letter to Rome Paul has not a little to say about it. In i. 24 he speaks of men dishonouring their bodies by giving them over to sin. In vi. 6 he speaks of 'the body of sin,' by which he means that sin has its seat and stronghold in the body. In vi. 12 he refers to the mortality of the body, and warns against sin being allowed to reign in it; which implies, of course, that sin is still in it in the Christian. In vii. 24 he calls it 'this body of death,' because it is 'that part of the regenerate man which yet has to *die*; and the Apostle longs to be free from it *as such*' (Moule). In viii. 10, he again refers to this, and says that as the body is doomed to death it is 'as good as dead.' In viii. 11 he declares that the body will be immortalized. In viii. 13 we are called upon continuously to 'put to death the doings of the body.' In viii. 23 we are told that the body one day will be redeemed. 'The redemption-price is paid already; the redemption-liberation is to come' (Moule). But we are meanwhile invited to dedicate our bodies as a living sacrifice to God (xii. 1).

Our bodies are our means of expression, and our media of communication with that which is outside of ourselves. If I had not my body I could not be talking to you now, and without yours, you could not be listening to me. The body is the nexus between within and without, and can be the agent of either good or evil.

Have we realized how tremendous a part our bodies must play in our living, or failing to live, a true Christian life? By our members we serve either Sin or Righteousness. If we *present* the members of our body as *weapons of righteousness* to God, our lips will speak His message, our hands will do His work, our feet will run His errands, and all our activities will show forth His glory.

We are not 'to keep on yielding our members to sin,' but are, by an act (aorist) to 'yield ourselves to God'; and our great encouragement is in the fact that not the law, but divine grace, is the power under which we are placed (14).

Secondly, there is the illustration of

MASTER AND SERVANT (6:15-23)

Because in ch. v. 20 Paul had said, 'where sin abounded grace did much more abound,' the question arose (vi. 1): '*What then? Shall we continue in sin that grace may abound?*' That question is answered in ch. vi. 1-11. But arising out of that answer is another question: '*What then? Shall we sin because we are not under law, but under grace?*' (14, 15); and the Apostle proceeds now to answer this question in his second illustration of the believer's relation to the Risen Lord—the illustration of *Master and Servant*.

This is an intensely interesting paragraph, and here is the fullest exposition of the subject of which it treats. In the Greek of the New Testament there are six words which are translated *servant*, and the one used in this passage, *doulos*, is the lowest in the scale of servitude, and should be translated *slave*, or *bondslave*.

The word is of interest here for two reasons among others: *firstly*, because Paul is writing to a city which was full of slaves, and in which the very word stirred a sense of horror; and we may gather from the last chapter of this Epistle that some of the members of the church at Rome were slaves; and *secondly*, because in the New Testament this word is used upwards of thirty times of God's people, and Paul frequently speaks of himself as a 'bondslave of Jesus Christ' (i.1, *et. al.*). It is this application of it to Christians that would take the bitterness out of it for the Christian slaves at Rome.

Now observe how Paul uses this illustration to indicate the relation of believers to the Risen Lord. He begins by announcing a principle, namely that each of us is a slave to something or someone; that each of us chooses his own master; and that having made our choice we are under obligation to be loyal to the contract.

Going to the root of the matter, the Apostle says that there are only two possible masters, and each of us must choose the one or the other. These masters are *Sin* and *Obedience* personified, and each has something to offer us; *death* being the offer of Sin, and *righteousness* the offer of Obedience. This is what he says:

> 'Are you not aware that to render service and obedience to anyone is to be the slave of that person or power to which obedience is offered? And so it is here. You are either slaves of Sin, and the end before you death; or you are true to your rightful Master, and the end before you righteousness' (16).

This is as true today as it was when Paul wrote nineteen hundred years ago. Each of us has a master, bad or good; we have chosen him; and our allegiance is due to him. If you have chosen Sin to be your master, then serve it; but if you have chosen Christ to be your Master, then serve Him; but the one thing you are not allowed to do is to say that you belong to one master and yet serve another. Jesus said, 'no man can serve two masters'; and in this passage Paul says, 'while you were slaves to Sin, you were freemen in regard to Righteousness' (20). The opposite is also true, and so the Apostle continues, 'but now, as Christians, you are emancipated from Sin and enslaved to God' (22). Let us think as clearly about this as Paul did. A spy is a criminal who incurs death, because while appearing to serve one nation he is in the pay of another. But what shall be said of the person who professes to belong to Christ, and who yet serves Sin! But, is this not what most of us are doing, and we are here at this time to face the tragic fact, and to do something about it.

A young woman, who had been very much in the world, got converted, and when one of her old associates invited her to a ball, she declined, and when asked why, she replied, pointing to herself, 'This establishment is under entirely new management.' That is as it should be. We should be loyal to the Master we choose, and not wear the badge of one, and do the bidding of another.

How striking a phrase is that in verse 18, *'having been set free* from sin, *you have become slaves* of righteousness.' The only real freedom is in slavery to Christ. Tersteegen perfectly expressed this truth when he wrote:

> 'Oh, lightest burden, sweetest yoke;
>   It lifts, it bears my happy soul,
>   It giveth wings to this poor heart;
>   My freedom is Thy grand control.'

We, therefore, are bidden to yield ourselves to God.

Sanday and Headlam have paraphrased verse 19 in this way:

> 'Yours must be an undivided service. Devote the members of your body as unreservedly to the service of righteousness for progressive consecration to God, as you once devoted them to Pagan uncleanness and daily increasing licence.'

In concluding his illustration Paul points out that Sin pays wages, and that God pays no wages but bestows a 'gift.'

> 'The wages (rations) of Sin is death, but the free-gift of God is eternal life in Christ Jesus our Lord' (23).

The Christian life begins with a choice, continues on a course, and has a glorious consequence.

But the Apostle has one more illustration of the Christian's relation to the Risen Lord. The first was the relation to one another of *King and Subject,* the second, of *Master and Servant,* and now, the third is that of

HUSBAND AND WIFE (7:1-6)

This paragraph falls into two parts. In verses 1-3 is the *illustration,* and in verses 4-6 is the *application;* and in each part there are three details, and these respectively answer to one another. The details relate to (*a*) the marriage bond; (*b*) the bond dissolved; and (*c*) the second marriage.

The *illustration* states that a woman is bound by law to her husband as long as he lives; that when he dies 'she is discharged from the law concerning him'; and then she is free to contract another marriage.

The *application* follows these three details. Yet the passage is the subject of considerable controversy.

It is commonly said that the Apostle's application does not follow his illustration; that in the illustration it is the husband that dies, whereas in the application it is the wife. A devout and learned expositor has declared that Paul uses his metaphor inconsistently, but, he adds, 'the change, whatever its cause, leaves it unchanged as an illustration.'

But surely the Apostle knew what he was talking about, and had too much intelligence and spiritual insight to bungle his metaphor. If, as many think, he did so, considerable confusion must result, because the wrong application would contradict the teaching of chapter six.

When Paul says that a woman is bound by law to her husband as long as he lives, he does not mean that the law is her husband, and he does not mean that the law dies; but if this were conceivable, who or what would the second husband be?

So objectionable is this view in every respect that we must look for an interpretation which is congruous with the illustration, is consistent with the teaching of the previous chapter, and is in consonance with the spiritual facts of which the Apostle is speaking.

Two things are perfectly clear: first, that those represented by the woman *were never married to the Law;* and, in the second place, that *the Law never dies.*

Who, then, are the parties in this application?

The Wife represents our personality, *our Ego*, which is permanent.

The Husband represents what Paul calls our 'old man' (or self), all we are by nature morally and spiritually, our state before conversion.

The Death of the Husband is the crucifixion of our 'old
man' (or self) with Christ.

By this crucifixion, our Ego, that is, 'we ourselves,'
become dead to our unregenerate state.

The New Marriage tells of the union upon which the
converted man enters with the Risen Lord.

This is simply another way of stating what is so
emphatically taught in chapter six, and elsewhere in
Paul's Writings. It is not the Law that dies, and it is
not Sin that dies, but the believer in Christ's death
and resurrection dies to both.

Paul says:

> 'We know that our old self was crucified with
> Christ, so that . . . we might no longer be enslaved
> to sin' (vi. 6).
> 'You have died to the law through the body of
> Christ, so that you may belong to Another, to
> Him who has been raised from the dead' (vii. 4).
> 'I have been crucified with Christ; it is no longer
> I who live, but Christ who lives in me' (Gal. ii. 20).

This is what our profession of Christ means and
involves. It is what God reckons to be so, and we
also must reckon it to be so.

> 'The death Christ died He died to sin, once for
> all, but the life He lives He lives to God.
> 'So you also must consider yourselves dead to
> sin and alive to God in Christ Jesus' (vi. 10, 11).

We are related to the King for *warfare;* to the
Master, for *service;* and to the new Husband for
fruitfulness.

'Fruit' in the teaching of Paul is not the product of

Christian service, but the ingredients of Christian character.

> 'The fruit of the Spirit is love, joy, peace, patience, kindness, goodness, faithfulness, gentleness, self-control' (Gal. v. 22).

The 'fruit for God' that we must bear is the dedication which produces practical holiness.

Thus far we have considered the Principle of Holiness (vi. 1-11), and the Practice of Holiness (vi. 12-vii. 6); and now our attention is called to

THE PREVENTIVE OF HOLINESS (7:7-25)

This consists in *the activity within of sin and self*.

Chapter vii is the problem chapter of this Epistle. Students of it are not agreed upon Paul's application of the illustration in verses 4-6, of the Husband and Wife; but verses 14-25 of the chapter are still more a subject of controversy. Opinion is sharply divided as to whether the experience here described is that of a regenerate or of an unregenerate person. The arguments on both sides are full of interest and instruction, but the present occasion does not lend itself to a consideration of these. Personally, against the majority of commentators, I believe that in these verses Paul, as a regenerate man, is telling of an experience through which he had passed, and through which very many Christians have passed, and are passing.

As in this Epistle it is the intention of the Apostle to give as comprehensive a view as is possible of the factors which, in thought and action, constitute Christianity, we may reasonably expect to find here, in constructive form, truths which appear in other of his Epistles, and these other references throw much light on what he says here.

In 1 Corinthians there are two verses which we may regard as the key to verses 7-25 of Romans vii. These are 1 Cor. ii. 14, and iii. 1, which read:

> 'The natural man receiveth not the things of the Spirit of God; for they are foolishness to him; neither can he know them, because they are spiritually discerned.'

> 'And I, brethren, could not speak unto you as unto spiritual, but as unto carnal, even as unto babes in Christ.'

That is an analysis of men which is exhaustive; and so there is no fourth class. The three classes are:

> the *natural* man (*psychikos*); the *carnal* man (*sarkikos*); the *spiritual* man (*pneumatikos*).

Each of us here, and everyone everywhere, is in one or other of these categories, and no one is in any two of them.

We are either '*natural*,' that is, in a state of nature, unregenerate; or we are '*carnal*,' that is, regenerate but not yielded to God—the word '*carnal*' is never used to describe an unregenerate person, but always refers to a Christian not delivered from the power of the flesh—or we are '*spiritual*,' that is, a Christian justified by God, and yielded to Him.

Now it seems to me that in this part of the Roman Epistle Paul brings to our notice these three classes. In ch. vii. 7-13, quite clearly he is speaking of himself in his unregenerate or '*natural*' state; in verses 14-25 of this same chapter he is, I believe, speaking of himself in a regenerate but '*carnal*' state; and in ch. viii. 1-17 he is explaining what is meant by the yielded or '*spiritual*' state. These states answer to the history of Israel, first in Egypt, then in the Wilderness, and finally in the Land. This gives a comprehensiveness and completeness to the teaching on this subject which is illuminating and challenging.

Today let us look at the first two of these states, the '*natural*,' and the '*carnal*,' and, God willing, to-morrow we shall consider the '*spiritual*' state, and also the believer's prospect of and in another world.

The subject is the *Preventive of Holiness*, and we have said that this consists in *the activity within of Sin and of Self*. The activity of *Sin* is dealt with in verses 7-13, and of *Self*, in verses 14-25. Look first of all at

ROMANS 6-8

The Activity of Sin (7:7-13)

Paul had said, 'You are not under law but under grace' (vi. 14), and as this might lead some to mis-interpret the nature and function of the Law from which the believer has been delivered, the Apostle here, in a passage intensely personal, vindicates the Law, and condemns himself. Earlier in the Epistle he had said that 'through the law comes knowledge of sin' (iii. 20), and now he will prove that; and he does so by showing the relation of Law to Sin.

Two things here should be carefully noted: first, that the passage is as definitely *autobiographical* as are Augustine's *Confessions*, and Bunyan's *Grace Abounding;* clearly Paul is speaking about himself; and secondly, that the tenses throughout the passage relate to the *past*. The Apostle says: 'I *knew* not'; 'sin *having taken* occasion by the commandment *worked-out* in me every lust'; 'I *was-alive*'; 'I *died*'; 'sin *deceived* me'; sixteen such tenses occur in verses 7-13,

and they signify that Paul is speaking of a past and
not of a present experience. He says that, so far from
the law being sin (7), it was to him the revealer and
occasion of sin. In his unregenerate childhood days
he did not know sin to be sin; but later, when he made
acquaintance with the Law, he realized that what
had seemed *innocent* was in reality *evil*. As soon as he
came up against the Law, sin which had been dormant
in him 'sprang into life,' and, he says, 'I died; con-
sciously I became a sinner, and realized that I had
no true life in me.' With the sense of guilt, the sense
of its penalty appeared.

This was true of Paul, and it is true of us. It is
when the Law says to us, 'thou shalt not,' that something in us rebels, and says, 'I will.' You tell a child
not to read a certain book, or not to look in a certain
cupboard, and immediately he will want to do both.
By nature we want our own way, not God's; and we
are made to realize this when we are confronted with
the law of God's will. The Law is 'holy, and just, and
good,' and it shows us that we are unholy, and un-
righteous, and evil. It is this that makes all the
resolutions of the unconverted man so hopeless; he
is trying to do and to be something which he has
no power to do or to be. I wonder if this is the case
of anyone to whom I am speaking!

It is made clear, then, that holiness is impossible
in the unregenerate. But it is now to be seen that it is
also impossible where there is

The Activity of Self (7:14-25)

Practically all students of this portion of the Epistle
are agreed that it is autobiographical, that Paul is

relating an experience which had been or was his own; but as to the time and nature of that experience students are in disagreement.

There are two distinct views. One is that Paul is here telling of an experience he had *before his conversion,* the experience of an unregenerate man struggling with the Law. The other view is that Paul is relating an experience he had *after his conversion* and before he entered upon the experience related in chapter eight; or, as some think, it is the experience of which the Apostle was then conscious, a conflict of self with self, of which any Christian may be sensible.

Now, two things here should be carefully noted: first, that the tenses are all *presents,* and no longer *pasts;* and secondly, that Paul is here engaged in a struggle with himself. The pronouns 'I,' 'my,' and 'me' occur forty times, but there is no reference to the Holy Spirit.

In verses 7-13 we see Paul in Egypt, but in verses 14-25 we see him in the Wilderness, yet longing for the Land, which in ch. viii he reaches. In these verses he is no longer 'natural,' as he was in verses 7-13, but he plainly says that he is 'carnal,' and, as we have already said, that word is never used of an unregenerate person. What we get in this paragraph is *not Christian experience, but the experience of a Christian.*

First of all, Paul shows his inability to keep himself from doing that of which he disapproves (14-17); then, he shows his inability to do that of which he does approve (18-20); and finally, he states the conclusion to which his experience drove him (21-25).

Whatever may be one's interpretation of these verses, so far as Paul is concerned, it is painfully

evident that they reflect the experience of a multitude
of truly regenerated people, many of whom deeply
deplore their failure to overcome evil, and to accomplish
good.

The reason for this unhappy experience may be
said to be threefold. First, the failure to grasp and
reckon upon the truth of ch. vi, that in Christ's death
we died, and in His resurrection we rose to 'newness
of life.' To many Christians that teaching is just
'double Dutch,' that is, it is unintelligible; and yet all
such would readily assent to the fact that 'unless a
grain of wheat falls into the earth and dies, it remains
alone; but if it dies, it bears much fruit' (John xii. 24).
A fundamental fact, alike in the realms of nature and
of grace, is that there must be death if there is to be
life. Where that truth is believed, and continuously
reckoned upon, the experience of Rom. vii. 14-25 is
impossible.

In the second place, this conflict is due to the fact
that the Self which is not reckoned to be dead is ever
active. Our Ego, our personality, is under the
dominion of the old unregenerate and unregenerable
Self, which Paul calls 'the old man'; or it is under the
dominion of the Spirit. In our passage there is no
reference to the Spirit, and so Self largely holds the
field, though it meets with the resistance of what
Paul calls his 'inward man,' that is, his regenerate Self,
but the battle goes sorely against him, and against
all who are in such a state.

In the third place, the breakdown of a Christian
is due to the fact that the Holy Spirit is not in control
of the whole life, within and without. There cannot
be civil conflict when the Spirit is regnant; but where

this is not so, all our faculties are at war; mind, and conscience, and emotion, and will are at loggerheads with one another.

Is this not the experience of many of you who have no doubt about your having been born-again? Let it not for a moment be supposed that the experience reflected in these verses is what God intends for His people. The cry here is not for pardon because of guilt, but for deliverance from bondage, and it is a cry which will not go unheard.

The Law which is 'holy, and just, and good' is also exacting and condemning; but by the death and resurrection of Christ on our behalf, we are delivered from it as an accuser and condemner.

> Free from the law, oh, happy condition.
> Jesus hath bled, and there is remission!
> Cursed by the law, and bruised by the Fall,
> Grace hath redeemed us once for all.
>
> Children of God! oh, glorious calling!
> Surely His grace will keep us from falling;
> Passing from death to life at His call,
> Blessed Salvation once for all.

And now to summarize. The subject of chs. vi-viii is *The Christian Life* in its *present* and *future*. In this world it should be characterized by holiness, and this is the theme of chs. vi. 1-viii. 17, where four aspects of the subject are expounded. First, the *Principle of Holiness,* which is in *the believer's mystical identification with Christ in His Death and Resurrection*. Secondly, the *Practice of Holiness,* which involves, on the part of the believer, *a recognition of and abandonment to the new relations* emerging from his identification with Christ, the relations of a *Subject to a King;* of a *Bondslave to a Master;* and of a *Wife to a Husband.* Thirdly, the *Preventive of Holiness,* which is found in *the activity within of Sin, and of Self.* That is the point we have now reached, and two things remain for our consideration; namely, the *Power of Holiness,* which is revealed as in *the unhindered dominion in the believer of the Holy Spirit;* and then, the theme of the believer's *Glorification,* which will be the crown and consummation of our redemption. These two matters are the subject of ch. viii, and are yet to be considered.

The truths unfolded in these three chapters (vi-viii) are the profoundest and sublimest in the New Testament, and a believing apprehension of them will bring any of us, and all of us, into an experience of God in Christ which, short of the final redemption, is the consummation of our salvation.

> 'Not under law, I'm now under grace,
> Sin is dethroned, and Christ takes its place.
> Glory be to God.'

The subject of chs. vi. 1-viii. 17 is *Sanctification,* the third great theme of the first division of this Epistle, and the Apostle Paul deals with the subject in four sections, which expound the *Principle,* the *Practice,* the *Preventive,* and the *Power* of Holiness. The first three of these we have considered, and now we are to contemplate the teaching on the *Power of Holiness* in ch. viii. 1-17.

Before doing so let us briefly survey the chapter as a whole. The subject of *Sanctification,* or *Holiness,* is the topic of verses 1-17; and from this the Apostle proceeds to the consideration of his fourth and last great theme in this doctrinal division of the Epistle, namely, *Glorification,* which is surveyed in verses 12-30; after which having expounded the *Philosophy of Salvation* under the topics *Condemnation, Justification, Sanctification,* and *Glorification,* Paul summarizes the whole of these eight chapters in a *Triumphant Song* (31-39).

Three things, then, invite our attention now: first, *the Revelation of the Power of Holiness;* secondly, *the Glorious Future of the Children of God Beyond this Life;* and thirdly, *the Eternal Security of the Believer in the Love of God.*

First, then:

THE POWER OF HOLINESS (8:1-17)

This is revealed to be the *Unhindered Dominion of the Spirit of God in the Believer.*

In ch. vii. 7-13 we are shown a '*natural man*'; in vii. 14-25, a '*carnal man*'; and here, in viii. 1-17, a '*spiritual man.*' In the first section the individual is in *Egypt;* in the second, he is in the *Wilderness;* and in the third, he is in the *Land.* The first is illustrated by Lazarus *dead in the grave;* the second, by Lazarus *alive, but bound* hand and foot with grave-clothes; and the third, by Lazarus *alive and free.*

Moses told the Israelites that God brought them out of Egypt that He might bring them into the Land, but many of them never entered the Land; they died in the Wilderness. In like manner, between Rom. vii. 7-13 and viii. 1-17, one may remain in vii. 14-25. It is perilously possible for a Christian to stick *between Calvary and Pentecost.* Jacob, between *Bethel* and *Peniel,* between his conversion and his full dedication to God, wasted twenty years in *Padan-aram.*

It is tragically actual that many who have come out of Egyptian bondage have never gone into Canaan blessing. Is it not true that very many Christians have never shed their grave-clothes? There is the smell of the tomb about them all the time. But we are here now, to get into our royal robes.

The importance of this section of Romans viii cannot possibly be exaggerated, because here is the very heart-secret of Christian experience, and of the true experience of Christians. The section should be studied with Galatians v. 13-25, which treats of the same subject, and which was written a little earlier in the same year as was the Letter to Rome. The attentive reader of these two portions of Holy Scripture will recognize that the subject of both is *the Flesh and the Spirit in the Believer,* and it is of the utmost importance that we understand the meaning and use of these terms.

THE SPIRIT

In Rom. viii. 1-17 the word '*spirit*' occurs 17 times, and the reader of the passage in the Authorized and Revised Versions will be puzzled to know what is meant by the word, because in the Authorized it is spelt fourteen times with a capital 'S,' and three times with a small 's' (10, 15, 16); but in the Revised in seven instances the 'S' is a capital, and in ten instances it is small. It can be assumed that when the 's' is small it is the *human spirit* that is referred to, and when it is a capital, the reference is to the *Holy Spirit.* Which, then, of these Versions is correct? Of that each reader must judge for himself, because men of equal scholarship and spiritual insight differ on the subject, but the difference is not so great as at first sight it may appear, because as the Apostle is addressing Christians only, the *human spirit* is viewed as being under the control of the *Holy Spirit.* Bishop Handley Moule takes the majority of the references to be to the *Holy Spirit,* and this is the view we adopt.

More is said in this portion about the Holy Spirit than anywhere else in the New Testament, except in our Lord's Upper Room Discourse (John xiv-xvi). In ch. vii where the *Preventive of Holiness* is discussed, there is no reference whatever to the Holy Spirit; but when the Apostle reaches the point where he can say, 'I thank God through Christ Jesus our Lord,' he is ready to tell his readers where the true and only *Power of Holiness* lies. It is in the indwelling Spirit, made regnant in the believer by faith. From the darkness and dampness of chapter vii the Apostle emerges into the clear and comforting truths of chapter viii. He passes from the prostration of defeat to the promise and provision of victory; from depression to delight, and from a sigh to a song.

But in this portion, as in Galatians v, there is another word, the meaning of which we must know if we are to understand these Scriptures and ourselves. It is

THE FLESH

This word, as used in Scripture, has many meanings, one of which is Paul's use of it metaphorically, as in the passage before us. Here, and elsewhere in the Pauline Epistles, it signifies either *the state of man unregenerate,* or '*in the regenerate, the state of that element of the being which still resists grace*' (Moule). It is in this latter sense that the Apostle uses it in these seventeen verses, where it occurs thirteen times. It is employed, therefore, not in a literal, but in a moral sense. The 'flesh' is our unregenerate and unregenerable fallen nature. For the believer it was put to death on the Cross, but the death was judicial and not actual, and so Paul says, 'reckon ye yourselves to be dead indeed unto sin, but alive unto God through Jesus Christ our Lord' (vi. 11).

THE FLESH AND THE SPIRIT

These, then, are the two powers that are ever claiming us for themselves.

When we became Christians this old nature was not eliminated. It was very active in the Galatians, and Paul asks them, 'Are ye so foolish? Having begun in the Spirit, are ye now perfecting yourselves in the flesh?'; and later in the same Epistle he says,

> 'the flesh lusteth against the Spirit, and the Spirit against the flesh, for these are contrary the one to the other, so that ye may not do the things that ye would' (v. 17).

In every unregenerate person there is but one nature, his fallen nature; but in every Christian there are two, his fallen self which was judicially put to death when Christ died, and his new regenerate nature which was secured for him by Christ's resurrection, and imparted to him at the moment of his regeneration.

If the 'flesh' had ceased to exist in us it could never have been said that it 'lusts against the Spirit'; nor, 'if we walk in the Spirit we shall not fulfil the lust of the flesh' (Gal. v). This old self is ever with us, and is ready to leap into activity again should the restraint

of faith in the will and power of Christ to overcome
it by the Holy Spirit be removed. Does not the
experience of each of us bear witness to this fact?

If the old self-nature which we inherited from the
Fall, actually died in us at the time of our conversion,
the first seventeen verses of Romans eight can have
no meaning. What the Apostle is here insisting upon
is that a Power is given to us, the Holy Spirit, by
Whom, if faith be present and continuous, the power
of self is negatived; it is annulled, that is, it is put
out of business. Sin is not dead, but we are to reckon
ourselves to be dead to it. When Peter walked on
the water the power of gravitation did not cease to
exist, but the operation of a greater law rendered it,
for the time being, inoperative; but as soon as Peter
put himself from under the new law, the old law again
asserted itself, and he began to sink. Now 'the law of
the Spirit of life in Christ Jesus made us (at the time
of our conversion) free from the law of sin and death,'
so that no longer are we to 'walk after the flesh, but
after the Spirit.' If the Holy Spirit, trusted by us,
cannot enable us to live a life of continuous victory
over indwelling sin, then Christianity is a failure and
a farce. But it is *not* a failure and a farce, for Paul
triumphed, and if he did, we can; and the Spirit
Who can give us victory for a single hour, can give
us victory every hour. The chapter which begins
with 'no condemnation' shows us that there need be
no defeat.

But victory is not inevitable. We must carry some
responsibility for our sanctification. The very exist-
ence of this Convention is evidence of this fact. God's
Provision must be trusted if we are to triumph. What

ROMANS 6-8

is ours by covenant must become ours by appropri-ation. What we *are* by and in Christ, we are to *become* by the indwelling Holy Spirit. The Flesh and the Spirit cannot be on the throne of our life at the same time, but one or other of them *must* be, and our responsibility is to say which of them *shall* be.

Justification is by faith, and not by struggle, and, in like manner, sanctification is not by struggle but by faith. *Faith* is one of the keywords of this Epistle, occurring over sixty times. It is the hand that takes what God offers; it is the faculty that believes what God says; it is the step that follows where God leads. 'Without faith it is impossible to please God.'

If we 'walk after the flesh,' it is because we have not faith. We may recite every day of our life, 'I believe in the Holy Ghost,' but if we do not 'walk after the Spirit,' we do not believe in Him. 'If we live in the Spirit, let us also walk in the Spirit,' and if we 'walk in the Spirit, we shall not fulfil the desire of the flesh.'

We are not to try to convert the 'flesh,' but rather, to recognize that it has been crucified; and because this is a truth of revelation, it ought to become one of experience.

THE HOLY SPIRIT

This eighth chapter of Romans is the *locus classicus* of Paul's teaching on the subject of the Holy Spirit, there being about twenty references to Him here, and some understanding of these is necessary if our sancti-fication is to be genuine and progressive.

It is made abundantly clear that the *Power of Holiness* is not a mere influence, but a Divine Person.

He is related to God, and to Christ, as being One of a Trinity (ver. 9). He is the *'Spirit of life'* (2), in that He is both the Giver and the Sustainer of life, to and in the believer. By Him our principle of conduct is regulated, which is spoken of here as *walking after Him* (4). His 'mind' is referred to, which, if the believer choose it, he will find to be 'life and peace' (6). It is stated that the believer is the sphere of the Spirit's indwelling, and that the Spirit is the Sphere of the believer's life (9). It is affirmed that if one 'has not the Spirit of Christ,' he is not a Christian at all (9). It is said that at last, at the resurrection, the Spirit will 'quicken our mortal bodies' (11). We are told that only by the Spirit can we progressively 'put to death the doings of the body,' and, in consequence, 'live' (13). It is revealed that the Spirit guides all who are truly subject in thought, word and deed to the rule of God's will (14). He is called the 'Spirit of adoption,' whereby the believer has the privilege and right to call God 'Abba, Father' (15). And, not to go further at present than these seventeen verses, it is said that the Divine Spirit bears witness with our human spirit that we are God's children, and heirs of God and of Christ (16, 17).

It is He, not It, Who within us antagonizes the 'flesh,' and, if we will but let Him, He will render it impotent as a principle and power of life.

> Life immortal, heaven descending,
> Lo! my heart the Spirit's shrine;
> God and man in oneness blending,
> Oh, what fellowship is mine!
> Full salvation!
> Raised in Christ to life divine.

But this wonderful revelation of the personality and power of the Spirit also warns us against thinking of Him apart from Christ, so making *a doctrine of the Spirit* which is the characteristic of a spurious Pentecostalism. Christ came to reveal and glorify the Father, and the Spirit has come to reveal and glorify Christ. His being in us, is Christ in us. 'Our experimental proof of the Spirit's fulness is that Christ to us is all.' Paul but teaches what Christ Himself declared when He said of the Spirit:

> 'He will not speak on His own authority, but whatever He hears He will speak. . . . He will glorify Me, for He will take what is Mine, and declare it to you' (John xvi. 13, 14).

There is no advance from Christ to the Spirit, but there is a perilous decline where the attempt is made to give the Spirit prominence over Christ. When Jesus said:

'I will not leave you desolate; I come to you.' He was referring to the advent of the Holy Spirit; so that the Spirit's coming to the Church was Christ's coming, and the Spirit's presence in the Church, and in the Christian, is Christ's presence.

And now we come to the last of Paul's four themes:

GLORIFICATION
Romans 8:12-30

In the consideration of *The Christian Life*, the Apostle views it first of all in the *present,* and then, in the *future*. In the present its characteristic is *Holiness* and in the future its consummation will be *Glory*. In chapter viii, verses 12-17 the one subject is con-

cluded and the other is commenced, and this shows
how intimately connected these subjects are.

In these verses (12-30) relating to coming Glory,
three things claim our attention: 1st: the *Promise* of it
(12-17); 2nd: the *Expectation* of it (18-27); and 3rd:
the *Certainty* of it (28-30).

THE PROMISE OF COMING GLORY (8:12-17)

Paul says that 'the Spirit bears witness with our
spirit that we are children of God; and if children
—children by *birth*, as well as by *adoption*—then *heirs,*
heirs of God, and *fellow-heirs* with Christ, provided we
suffer-together, in order that we may also be glorified-
together (16, 17).   It is the word '*heirs*' that is important here, and which indicates that the Apostle
has now the future in view.   An *heir* is one who will
come into an *inheritance*, one who does not as yet
possess his estate.   As children born into God's family,
we shall one day enter into the full possession of His
Kingdom.   Paul speaks of it as 'the inheritance
among all them that are sanctified'; and says that
our being 'sealed with the Holy Spirit of promise' is
'an earnest of our inheritance'; and Peter speaks of it
as 'an inheritance incorruptible, and undefiled, and
that fadeth not away, reserved in heaven for (us).'
What this will be we cannot tell, for the extent and
wonder of it are beyond our present comprehension,
but it is promised to all who are God's children by
regeneration, and only to such, for there is no heirship
where there is no sonship.

In this world an heir does not enter upon his
inheritance until the present possessor of it deceases,
but in the case of the believer, God is not a dying

testator, but the ever-living bestower of His goods on His children.

It is at this point that Paul introduces a subject which is to dominate the rest of this chapter, namely that *suffering is the path to glory.* We are heirs of God and of Christ,

> 'if-indeed we-suffer-together,
> that also we-may-be-glorified-together' (17).

There are only five words in this statement, as Paul dictated it, and two of them are verbs, '*to-suffer-with*,' and '*to-glorify-with*'; the first of which occurs only twice in the New Testament, and the second, only here. But what is important to notice is that the reference to 'suffering-with' is in the present tense, and the reference to 'being-glorified-with' is in the aorist tense, which means that, whereas the suffering is continuous in this life, the being-glorified is instantaneous and complete in the next life. The suffering referred to is not that which is the lot of all men, but that which is due to our union with Christ, to our being Christians. With this in mind let us follow Paul as he now speaks of

THE EXPECTATION OF COMING GLORY (8:18-27)

This expectation is stimulated and intensified by the suffering referred to. The Apostle was very competent to speak on this subject, because he had been, was, and was yet to be, a great sufferer for Christ.

Comparing himself with others, he says that his were

> 'far greater labours, far more imprisonments, with
> countless beatings, and often near death. Five times
> I received at the hands of the Jews forty lashes less
> one. Three times I have been beaten with rods;

once I was stoned. Three times I have been shipwrecked; a night and a day I have been adrift at sea; on frequent journeys, in danger from rivers, danger from robbers, danger from my own people, danger from Gentiles, danger in the city, danger in the wilderness, danger at sea, danger from false brethren; in toil and hardship, through many a sleepless night, in hunger and thirst, often without food, in cold and exposure. And, apart from other things, there is the daily pressure upon me of my anxiety for all the churches' (2 Cor. xi. 23-28).

If any of us had endured a third of these sufferings, we would have written a portly volume about it, and have expected an enriching royalty from our publisher; but about it all the Apostle says,

> 'I consider that the sufferings of this present time are not worth comparing with the glory that is to be revealed to us' (18).

And in another great passage he says,

> 'Though our outward man is being brought to decay, yet the inward is being renewed day by day. For the momentary lightness of our tribulation an eternal weight of glory, excessively surpassing, works out' (2 Cor. iv. 16, 17).

How wonderful it would be if this truth could be impressed upon every suffering Christian in China, and Russia, in Korea, and Malaya, in Europe and elsewhere, for it is a truth that

> 'Sometime, when all life's lessons have been learned,
> And sun and stars for evermore have set,
> The things which our weak judgments here have spurned,
> The things o'er which we grieved with lashes wet,
> Will flash before us, out of life's dark night,
> As stars shine most in deeper tints of blue;
> And we shall see how all God's plans are right,
> And how what seemed reproof was love most true.

'But not today. Then be content, poor heart.
God's plans like lilies pure and white unfold;
We must not tear the close-shut leaves apart,
Time will reveal the calyxes of gold.
And if, through patient toil, we reach the land
Where tired feet, with sandals loosed, may rest,
Where we shall clearly see and understand,
I think that we will say, "*God knew the best.*"'

Well, having made this statement about coming glory, the Apostle shows the need for it, and declares the certainty of it, in respect first of *Creation*, and then, of the *Christian*.

First, then, is

(a) *The Expectation of the Creation* (8:18-22)

This is a marvellous passage, and would require angelic eloquence to do it justice. The Apostle says that all Creation, which mysteriously came under the curse of man's Fall, is, at the end, to share in man's redemption; it is to be completely changed, and to enter on 'an endless æon of indissoluble life and splendour.' Many and great are the beauties and uses of nature, but in it also are dreadful and devastating forces, forces which act with impersonal ferocity. There are flood and flame, typhoon and tornado, blizzard and blight, volcanic eruption and cyclonic destruction, terrifying lightning and thundering avalanche, cruel oceans, fearsome deserts, and threatening mountains.

Also there are savage beasts, poisonous reptiles, loathsome insects, horrible fishes, and dangerous birds. There is a depravity of nature which is unwitting, and, as the Apostle says, 'unwilling'; but all this will be changed.

Very graphic is the Apostle's declaration that all creation as though listening for the footfall of God, is *'waiting-with-outstretched-head'* for the day when redemption shall be accomplished, when it, too, 'shall be delivered from the bondage of corruption into the glorious liberty of the children of God.'

It is when this takes place that 'the hills shall break forth into singing, and all the trees of the field shall clap their hands'; that 'the wilderness and the solitary place shall be glad, and the desert shall rejoice and blossom as the rose'; that 'the wolf shall dwell with the lamb, and the leopard shall lie down with the kid, and the calf, and the young lion, and the fatling together; . . . and the suckling child shall play on the hole of the asp, and the weaned child shall put his hand on the adder's den; and they shall not hurt nor destroy' (Isa. xi. 6-9). Then will the whole creation 'groan and travail in pain' no more. That day is coming, and it may be nearer than we think.

From this aspect of his subject the Apostle passes on to the consideration of

(b) *The Expectation of the Christian* (8:23-27)

The Creation groans, and the Christian groans; the Creation eagerly waits, and the Christian eagerly waits; the Creation awaits the believer's full redemption, and the Christian awaits his own full redemption, the redemption of the body; deliverance is promised to the Creation, and deliverance is the sure prospect of the Christian. There is this difference however, that whereas the longing of the Creation is without sensibility or emotion, the longing of the Christian is

ROMANS 6-8

in the full consciousness of a rational and moral being who has been regenerated by the Spirit of God, and who is living in confident assurance that 'He Who has begun a good work in us, will perfect it until, and in, the day of Jesus Christ.'

It would be more correct to say that 'we are saved *in* hope,' than *by* it; and this just means, that 'when we believed we accepted a salvation whose realization was future, and could therefore be enjoyed only in the hope we felt in view of it.' This hope, we learn from other references, is that of Christ's Return, when our regenerated selves will be given trans-figured bodies, and the work of redemption be thus completed.

The Christian's hope is not that the world will be converted, but that the Lord will come again, and complete, first in His Church, and then in the earth, what He died on the Cross to accomplish. Here and now the work is imperfect, and must remain so until the Advent. It is not active sinfulness that must remain, but what Paul calls 'weakness,' or 'infirmity,' all that encumbers and obstructs our 'patient expecta-tion'; and in this he includes our *prayers*.

He says, what surely we are all aware of in our own devotional life, that 'we do not know how to pray as we ought.' The spirit of our prayers may be right, but, too often, what I may call the *text* of them is mistaken. When that demon-possessed man who was healed by Jesus, 'begged Him that he might be with Him,' the motive was good, but the request was refused; instead, Jesus sent him home to tell his friends of the mercy that had been shown to him. Paul, who had what he called 'a thorn in the flesh,' prayed that it might be removed, but his request was not granted; instead, God gave him grace to endure it. Monica prayed that her profligate son Augustine might not go to Rome, where he would find a cesspool of iniquity to encourage him in sin, but thither her wayward boy went, and the move proved a step on the way to Milan where he was converted. Our requests may be mistaken, but if our heart is right we cannot say that our prayers have been unanswered.

'We ask for strength that we might achieve; we are made weak that we might obey. We ask for health that we might do greater things; we are given infirmity that we might do better things. We ask for power that we might have praise of men; we are given weakness that we might feel our need of God. We ask for all things that we might enjoy life; we are given life that we might enjoy all things.' It may be that we receive little of what we ask for, but we yet may receive all that we hope for.

And how does this come about? Our portion tells us: 'The Spirit Himself intercedes for us with sighs too deep for words,' and this intercession for the saints is 'according to the will of God' (26, 27). The real secret of a true prayer life is found in the fact that both the Spirit and the Risen Lord are praying with us, and for us, and as their prayers *must* be answered, the believer knows that his groaning will cease, and that he will enter into glory.

Having called attention, relative to our Glorification, to the *Promise* and the *Expectation* of it, the Apostle now crowns the subject by presenting in immortal words,

The Certainty of Coming Glory (8:28-30)

In verse 26, relative to prayer, he says, '*we know not*,' but here, relative to a vaster subject, he says, '*we know*.' When he says, '*we know not*,' he refers to our *understanding*, but here he refers to our *faith*, for in no other way could 'we know that all things work together for good to them that love God, to them who are called according to His purpose.'

Our knowledge is by faith in God's Word, but in actual experience we have often found it difficult to believe what here is declared. Of course 'we know' that things *work*, that *all* things work, that all things *work-together*. So far we can go with steady tread; but at the next point, 'all things work-together *for good*,' there is a likelihood that we may falter. Indeed we may, and should entirely stop, for it is not true that 'all things work-together for good'; at least, this is not what the passage says. On the contrary, earlier in the Epistle, Paul says that 'the law works wrath' (iv. 15), and that 'sin works death' (vii. 13). Only within a certain limitation is it true that 'all things work-together for good,' and this limitation is, '*to them that love God*.' There is a sense in which every believer loves God, for we could not be Christians unless we did; yet, how many there are who have doubts about this declaration, notwithstanding their profession of saving faith. It would seem, then, that '*them that love God*' has a particular, and not merely a general significance. It would seem to refer to those Christians who are living in daily trustful fellowship with God, through Christ, by the Spirit; those to whom God's will is the law of their life; and who see all circumstances and happenings in which they have a share, in the light of His loving purpose for them. The Divine '*purpose*' embraces all Christians, but all Christians are not yielded to the Divine '*purpose*'; but to those who are, and who in this way show their love for God, 'all things work-together for good.' For all such, 'out of the eater comes forth meat, and out of the strong comes forth sweetness.'

Nourishment and satisfaction come out of what devours and desolates; the trustful find a blessing in the blast; for them swords are turned into plough-shares, and spears into pruning-hooks; peace emerges from conflict; vigour grows out of weakness; hope shines forth from despair as stars in the night; and rapture becomes the fair flower of anguish.

'*All things* work-together for good *to them that love God.*' The true lover of God finds that there is a compensation for every handicap, and a reward for every disability. He

'Climbs the rainbow through the rain,'

and discovers that seeming disaster becomes the shining way to sovereignty. Prison became this to Joseph, and Paul, and Bunyan; and in cruel captivity in Patmos, John received Visions which have enriched the Church of God for over nineteen hundred years. In our *social* life we have to *know* in order to *love*, but in our *spiritual* life we have to *love* in order to *know*.

That the 'purpose' of God for His people determines His providence relative to them, is made clear in what immediately follows in this portion.

> 'Those whom He foreknew He also predestined to be conformed to the image of His Son, ... and those whom He predestined He also called; and those whom He called He also justified; and those whom He justified He also glorified.'

What a golden chain of blessings — *predestined,*
conformed, called, justified, and *glorified;* and I would have
you observe that all the tenses are in the *past;* 'the
whole process is viewed as in its eternal completeness.
We *look back,* as it were, from the view-point of glory'
(Moule); and herein is the *assurance* of which I am
speaking. Everything from *predestination* before history
began, to *glorification* at its end is, in God's view,
already accomplished, and in the Church's experience
will be accomplished when her course on earth is
finished.

Profound mysteries lie embedded in this great
utterance, and theologians will continue to debate
them, but our obligation and privilege here and
now is to believe them, and to bow with devout
thanksgiving in His presence Who is our Alpha and
Omega.

With this verse 30, the doctrinal division of the
Epistle ends, and, as is the manner of the Apostle, the
whole of the preceding unfolding is summarized in
the remaining verses of the chapter (31-39); so let us
conclude by looking at this final rapturous passage.

SUMMARY Romans 8:31-39

FROM CONDEMNATION TO GLORIFICATION CELEBRATED
IN A TRIUMPHANT SONG (8:31-39)

We have said and seen that the first of the three
main divisions of this Epistle ends with chapter viii,
and that in unfolding the *Philosophy of Salvation* the
Apostle discusses four subjects: *Condemnation, Justifica-*
tion, Sanctification, and Glorification. At the end of the
first two subjects he summarizes his argument, tracing
Condemnation to Adam, and Justification to Christ.

He then proceeds to discuss *Sanctification,* and *Glorification,* and, this done, he summarizes the whole argument *from Condemnation to Glorification,* celebrating it in a *Triumphant Song.*

Surely this must be one of the most eloquent passages in all literature! Listen to it, in Tyndale's incomparable translation:

What shall we then say to these things?
If God be for us, who can be against us?
He that spared not His own Son,
But delivered Him up for us all,
How shall He not with Him
Also freely give us all things?

Who shall lay anything to the charge of God's elect?
God that justifieth?
Who is He that condemneth?
Christ that died? yea, rather that is risen again?
Who is even at the right hand of God?
Who also maketh intercession for us?

Who shall separate us from the love of Christ?
Tribulation? or distress? or persecution?
Or famine? or nakedness? or peril? or sword?
  As it is written:
  "For Thy sake we are killed all the day long;
  We are accounted as sheep for the slaughter."
Nay in all these things we are more than conquerors
Through Him that loved us.

For I am persuaded that
    Neither death, nor life,
    Nor angels, nor principalities, nor powers,
    Nor things present, nor things to come,
    Nor height, nor depth,
    Nor any other creature,
Shall be able to separate us from the love of God,
Which is in Christ Jesus our Lord.

ROMANS 6-8

We may divide this magnificent passage into two portions, and in the treatment of each the Apostle well-nigh exhausts thought and language. Both relate to the believer's Security, as assuring Glory, but the first (31-34) tells of the *Reality* of it; and the second (35-39) tells of the *Eternity* of it.

THE REALITY OF THE BELIEVER'S SECURITY (8:31-34)

'*What shall we then say to these things?*' What things? Everything that has gone before in this Epistle. The challenge is thrown out, '*Who can be against us?*' Oh, there are innumerable adversaries ever ready and eager to oppress the people of God. When Paul says '*Who can?*' he does not mean that there are none that can, but that there are none that can do so with any hope of success, because they have Almighty God to reckon with; and He, having given 'His own Son' to die for us, will not let His enemies damage the security of His people.

Having asked a question about *opposition,* and answered it, Paul now asks a question about *accusation,* and answers it.

Here I follow the punctuation which makes all the phrases in this paragraph *questions,* six in all. This reading gives dramatic force to the paragraph, and each question implies the answer of an emphatic '*No.*'

'*Who shall lay anything to the charge of God's elect?*' 'Who is he that condemneth?' No one can be condemned who is not charged, but the Apostle separates the two ideas, and answers the challenge about the 'charge' by asking, with incredulity, another question: 'Will the God who has justified His people bring a fatal "charge" against them?' Were that possible, justification would be of no avail. Sin may charge us, Satan may charge us, the law may charge us, our own conscience and heart may charge us, but if God has justified us—and He has, if we have believed—all accusers are silenced, for the charges are no longer valid.

But this notwithstanding, the Apostle asks the further question, 'Who is he that condemneth?' and for answer asks four other questions in rapid succession, questions which summarize the whole Christian Gospel. Will Christ condemn us Who died for us? No. Will Christ condemn us Who rose again for us? No. Will Christ condemn us Who is now at God's right hand for us? No. Will Christ condemn us Who is forever interceding for us? A thousand times 'No.' Christ's *crucifixion, resurrection, ascension,* and *intercession* make the condemnation of His people an utter impossibility. Both 'charge' and 'condemnation' are impossible, for both were accepted and discharged on Calvary by the Sinless Lamb of God. So

> 'Now are we free, there's no condemnation;
> Jesus provided a perfect salvation.'

The matter of the believer's security is as certain as God can make it.

And now the Apostle has something to say about

THE ETERNITY OF THE BELIEVER'S SECURITY (8:35-39)

Here another question arises, relating to the believer's *safety.* The answers to the previous one about the Reality of our *security,* all point to the *past* and the *present;* to what God by Christ has done, and is now doing for us. But what about the *future?* May it not

ROMANS 6-8

be that some hostile power will succeed in violently breaking the bond which unites us to the Lord, and on which both our justification and sanctification rest? With this in mind the Apostle asks:

'*Who shall separate us from the love of Christ?*'

Present *security* can be of little comfort to us if there is the possibility of future *separation*. But this challenge also Paul takes up. and with glowing eloquence puts the matter beyond dispute. He names seven angry personalities that bear a grudge at the bond uniting believers to Christ, and he asks, 'Can any one of these break the bond, and sever us from Christ?'

Here are the menacing powers:

Tribulation? Anguish? Persecution? Famine? Nakedness? Danger? Sword?

Can any of these separate us from Christ? Of all people Paul had the greatest right to ask such a question, because each of these troubles had attacked him (2 Cor. vi. 4-10; xi. 23-28; xii. 10), but no one of them, nor all of them together, had separated him from his Lord. The last one, the *sword*, had yet to come, but triumphantly Paul faced that also.

And now, before his final burst of God-inspired emotion, the Apostle gives his emphatic answer to the questions just asked. He says:

> '*But in all these things*—cruel oppression, acute pain, malignant pursuit, starvation, defencelessness, exposure to harm, and horrible death—in all these things *we more than overcome*—we are over-victorious, we gain a victory that is more than a victory— *through Him who loved us*' (37).

How can we '*more* than overcome'? Can one *more* than win? Oh, yes. One can obtain a victory on points; not that however, but an overwhelming defeat of the foe is in Paul's mind. This is what he means when he says elsewhere:

> On every side pressed hard,
>   But not hemmed in;
> Without a way,
>   But not without a by-way;
> Pursued,
>   But not abandoned;
> Thrown down,
>   But not destroyed
>   (2 Cor. iv. 8, 9. *Rotherham*).

We are not to come out of the fray saying, 'My! that was a narrow shave,' but with a dance, swinging Goliath's head in our hand.

And now follows a statement of Paul's own faith, wherein he spreads his wings and soars like an eagle right into the sun. He says:

> '*I am persuaded*'—assured, confident, convinced—no humming-and-hawing there, but a ringing confidence.

Paul is not expressing an *opinion*, but affirming a *conviction;* and one well-founded conviction is worth far more than ten thousand dubious opinions. You will never be a power until you *know* something on which you are prepared to stake your life.

Well, what is the substance of Paul's persuasion? Just this, that *there are no powers throughout the whole universe that are able to snap the bond between the Saviour and the believer.*

And here he summons the soul's adversaries in pairs, only to dismiss them.

ROMANS 6-8

The first pair represent *extremes of state—death,* and *life.* Can *death* separate us from Christ? No. Can *life?* which is often more difficult than death? No. Both these states can separate us from much, but not from Christ's love; therefore they are put aside to head a group of incompetents and impotents.

The second pair represent *superhuman intelligences —Angels,* and *Principalities,* and Paul adds *Powers,* the whole dominion of fallen spiritual hosts, against whom he says we wrestle. These are terrifying forces, but they are entirely unable to separate the Christian from Christ, for no one can come between us and Him but ourselves.

The third pair represent *all time which is ours—things present,* and *things to come,* 'the boundless field of circumstance and contingency.' The hardships of the present, and the uncertainties of the future are powerless to detach us from Him in Whom 'we live, and move, and have our being.'

The fourth pair represent *dimensions of space—height* and *depth.* These, with all that they hold of mystery and immensity, cannot break the bond between us and our Redeemer.

And lest in this mighty sweep of things, abstract and concrete, personal and impersonal, dimensional and temporal, visible and invisible, animate and inanimate, intellectual and insensible, incorporeal and physical, lest, all these notwithstanding, Paul should have omitted anything, he adds, '*nor any other created thing throughout all creation*' shall have the power to sunder us from 'the love of God which is in Christ Jesus our Lord.'

The Apostle strikes the deepest and sweetest note

when he speaks of the love of God which, in verse 35 is spoken of as 'the love of Christ,' and in ch. xv. 30, as 'the love of the Spirit.' This is the love of the Triune God, and is a love, not of sentiment or emotion, but of principle; a love unprovoked by us, and beyond our power to destroy. It is from this love that nothing and no one can separate us.

> 'Stronger His love than death or hell;
> Its riches are unsearchable;
> The first-born sons of light
> Desire in vain its depths to see,
> They cannot reach the mystery,
> The length, the breadth, the height.'

This first division of the Epistle which began in the midnight darkness of man's sin, ends in the blazing light of God's love. It began by showing us what we are by nature, and it ends by showing us what we may become by grace. It began with 'There is none that doeth good, no, not one,' and it ends with, 'We are more than conquerors through Him that loved us.' From the nadir of despair we are lifted to the zenith of triumph. If Christ is left to us nothing else matters. Hurtful though our enemies can be to us, we can snap our fingers at them, and say,

> 'I know beyond a shadow of a doubt that
> neither tribulation, nor distress, nor persecution,
> nor famine, nor nakedness, nor sword, nor
> death, nor life, nor principalities, nor powers,
> nor things present, nor things to come, nor height,
> nor depth, nor any other created thing—
> no one of these, nor all of them together, is
> able to separate me from the love of God, of
> which Christ is the embodiment. Glory be to the
> Father, and to the Son, and to the Holy Ghost.'
> > Amen, and Amen.

PHILOSOPHY OF BEHAVIOR
(Romans 12:1-15:13)

3

PATHS OF DUTY
(Romans 12-13)

THIS Epistle to the Romans is in three main divisions. In the first (i-viii), the subject is *Salvation*, in the widest possible sense, reaching from the *necessity for it in sin,* to the *consummation of it in Glory*. In the second division (ix-xi), the subject is the Divine *Providence and Purpose in the Calling of Israel*. And in the third division (xii-xvi), the subject is *Practical Christianity*.

The second division is a vital part of the whole Epistle, but for our present purpose we omit it, and pass from the *Doctrinal* to the *Practical* divisions; for, by so doing, we can see more clearly the relation to one another of *truth and life; of revelation and responsibility; of principles and practice; of religion and morality; of doctrine and duty; of redemption and behaviour.* Salvation as a Divine revelation is of no value unless it eventuates in character and conduct which are conformable to the purpose of the Redeemer.

Christianity is not merely or primarily a philosophy, but a quality of life, called 'eternal life'; and by 'eternal life,' is not meant a life which we shall enter upon beyond time, but a life to be lived here and now in all conceivable conditions and circumstances.

But it should be understood that not only are Salvation and Behaviour vitally related, but also that they are related in this order. Behaviour is not the root, but the fruit; not the foundation, but the superstructure; not the cause, but the effect. Belief precedes behaviour in every true unfolding of Christianity.

And now, having considered the mighty sweep of *Salvation* from *Sin to Glory*, let us turn our attention to *Christian Behaviour*, which fits into the doctrine, and embodies it.

This subject is unfolded in chapters xii-xv, and we may divide it into two main parts. The first of these points out *Paths of Duty* (xii-xiii); and the second sets forth *Principles of Action* (xiv-xv. 13); and each of these parts is rich with instruction for all who would live a victorious Christian life. First of all, then, let us consider *Paths of Duty* (xii-xiii).

Here we are told what our duty is, and how we can perform it. To begin with, *the fundamental conditions* of Christian living are indicated (xii. 1, 2), and then, *the manifold expressions* of it are detailed (xii. 3-xiii. 14).

THE FUNDAMENTAL CONDITIONS of Christian living are indicated in two profound verses which link together all that has already been said in the Epistle, and all that remains to be said.

> 'I exhort you therefore, brethren, by the compassions of God, to present your bodies a living sacrifice, holy, well-pleasing to God, which is your rational service. And fashion not yourselves to this age, but be transformed by the renewing of your mind, that you may prove what is the will of God, the good, and well-pleasing, and perfect (will)'.

The word '*therefore*' should be marked, which occurs, as we have said, at three critical points in the Epistle; in v. 1; viii. 1; and xii. 1. The first is the 'therefore' of *Salvation:* '*Therefore* being justified by faith, we have peace with God through our Lord Jesus Christ.' The second is the 'therefore' of *Sanctification:* 'There is *therefore* now no condemnation to them that walk not after the flesh, but after the Spirit.' And the third is the 'therefore' of *Service:* 'I exhort you *therefore* to present your bodies a living sacrifice.' There is no true service where there is not sanctification; and there is no sanctification where there is not salvation. This, then, is the spiritually organic order. Salvation is by the surrender of the *heart* to God; sanctification is by the surrender of the *will;* and service is by the surrender of the *body.* This being so, it must be evident that true sanctification and effective service are not inevitable; that there can be genuine salvation, in its first meaning, without them. Each of these stages is reached by faith, and each constitutes a spiritual crisis in the experience of the individual, because each is entered into by an act, which is followed by a spiritual development.

In these two verses we are told that the fundamental conditions of Christian living relate to what is *outward,* and to what is *inward* in our life. The *Outward Condition* is the *dedication of the body;* and the *Inward Condition* is the *renewal of the mind.*

The Dedication of the Body, which is *the outward condition* of Christian living is to be a definite and solemn act. In Paul's '*present your bodies,*' two things should be observed. First, that it is to be *an act;* the verb is in the tense which means to do something instantly and completely, and secondly, that the presentation is a *sacrificial act;* not propitiatory, but dedicatory; not a sin-offering, but a burnt-offering. The sacrifices of old were *dead*, but our sacrifice must be '*living*'; those of old were not always 'well-pleasing to God,' but the sacrifice of our body—brain, eyes, ears, tongue, hands, and feet—will be well-pleasing to Him. Such a dedication of the body is in harmony with the highest intelligence; Paul calls it '*rational*'; and we shall realize that it is this, when we recognize the place and function of the body in the Christian life.

The Renewal of the Mind, which is *the inward condition* of Christian living, is profoundly impressive. In but 27 words *a programme is presented; a process is unfolded;* and *a purpose is revealed.*

The Programme is: '*Be not conformed . . . but be transformed.*' These are the negative and positive aspects of the same thing, and they are mutually exclusive. Every 'age' has its own characteristics, but there are some things which are common to every age.

In Jude, verse 11, we read of '*the way of Cain,*' that is, *pride of intellect;* of '*the error of Balaam,*' that is, *the love of money;* and of '*the gainsaying of Korah,*' that is, *contempt of authority.* These three things—*rationalism, mammonism,* and *anarchism*—appear in every age, and to them, as well as to special features of our own age, we are not to be conformed. Our 'age' is not to be our fashion plate, because it is both false and fleeting.

The Process is: '*By the renewing of your mind.*'
The true safeguard against a sinful conformation is a spiritual transformation, and this will be a continuous experience. The dedication of the body is by *an act*, but the transformation of the mind is *a process;* and the process is both God's work, and ours.

ROMANS 12,13

Because our faculty of discernment functions faultily, it must be continuously renewed. The *will* that it should be so is ours, but the *work* is the Holy Spirit's (Titus iii. 5).

And *the Purpose* of this programme and process is, '*That we may prove what is the will of God, the good, and well-pleasing, and perfect will.*'

This, then, is the only foundation of a true Christian life, and all that follows rests upon it, and emerges from it. Following on the Fundamental Conditions, are

THE MANIFOLD EXPRESSIONS of Christian living. First of all the Apostle details *the various spheres* in which the Christian life must be lived (xii. 3-xiii. 7); he then discloses *the impelling power* of such a life (xiii. 8-10); and, finally, makes evident *the great incentive* to it (xiii. 11-14). Let us consider, then, first of all,

(i) THE VARIOUS SPHERES in which the Christian Life must be lived (12:3-13:7)

Here three Paths of Duty are set before us, which relate to the *Church* (xii. 3-13); to the *World* (xii. 14-21); and to the *State* (xiii. 1-7); and refer respectively to our *Religious*, our *Social*, and our *Civil duty*.

The Apostle introduces this great subject by calling upon us to form, as far as may be possible, a true estimate of ourselves (3). He says:

> '*Do not be high-minded above what it behoves you to be minded, but be minded so as to be sober-minded, as to each God has divided a measure of faith.*'

This is a most important statement, and requires of us more honest thinking than, perhaps, we have ever given to it. Self-estimate must be on one or other of three levels: *super*, above; *sub*, under; or *sane*, right. On the *super* level are the *superiority complex* people; and on the *sub* level are the *inferiority complex* people, and they are both off the right level. Generally speaking, we Christians think either too much of ourselves, or too little, and both estimates are bad for the Church, as well as for ourselves.

Self-admiration is pride and conceit, which is bad for oneself, unjust to others, and throws the machinery of Christian life and work out of gear.

On the other hand, *self-depreciation* neither honours God, encourages ourselves, nor blesses others. A sub-estimate of oneself unfits one for the work of life, and must not be mistaken for Christian humility. One of these parties should sing, 'Oh, to be nothing, nothing'; and the other should sing, 'Oh, to be something, something.' He who over-estimates himself will try to do what he cannot; and he who under-estimates himself will not try to do what he can; and in both cases the work is not done. In the Church, as in every business, there is manifold operation, and so there must be diversity of ability; there is therefore no room for *super* or *sub* estimation of oneself.

The bearing of this on what follows must be obvious, for by a right estimate of ourselves we shall be better able to fulfil our duty to the Church, to the World, and to the State.

Consider, then, what Paul says about

1. OUR DUTY TO THE CHURCH (12:4-13)

Here he speaks, first of all, of our *corporate* (4-8), and then, of our *individual responsibility* (9-13).

Our Corporate Responsibility (12:4-8)

This relates to the place and function of each believer in the Christian Church. Perhaps it may be said that never so much as now was it imperative to know what the New Testament means by the Christian Church. By likening the Church to a human body and its members (4), the Apostle is simply affirming that the Church is a Spiritual Organism, and not a human organization. The Christian Church is not the aggregate of all denominational churches, but the sum total of all believing individuals, men, women, and children. This is not the view of the present-day Movement for the Reunion of Christendom, which, in my view, because I believe it to be the New Testament view, would be an appalling disaster.

No, Paul says that all regenerated people constitute the Body of Christ, and that in this Body each has a place and a part to fulfil.

If, during these nineteen hundred years, believers had kept this steadily in mind, and had acted upon it, many a sad chapter of Church history would never have been written. What each of us must realize is, *first*, that no one of us has all the gifts; *secondly*, that each of us has some gift, or gifts; and *thirdly*, that all the gifts are necessary if the whole Body is to function properly.

One colour does not make light; one branch does not make a tree; one worker does not make a firm; one flower does not make a garden; one tree does not make a forest; one wave does not make a tide; one star does not make a constellation; one grain does not make a harvest; one instrument does not make an orchestra; one limb does not make a body; and so one member does not make a Church.

Relative to the Body of Christ this is what Paul is insisting on here. Unity, not uniformity, characterizes the Christian Church, and in this unity is vast diversity. If each of us did what Christ has placed us in His Body to do, and recognized with appreciation the functions of others, the Church would be a power in the world, instead of being 'by schisms rent asunder, and by heresies distressed.' In the true Church no two believers are endowed alike, but there is no one who is not endowed.

To illustrate this, the Apostle selects seven gifts, four of which are exercised more publicly, and three, more privately, but all are used for the benefit of the whole Church. These gifts cover a wide field of ministry, and exhibit wide variety; yet they are but a small selection of the wealth of ability which Christians have.

The gifts specified are: *Prophesying,* that is preaching; *Serving,* which relates to the business and administrative work of the Church; *Teaching,* that is, interpreting revealed truth; *Exhorting,* that is, appealing to the conscience and will, rather than to the intellect, and which is more the work of the evangelist than of the teacher; *Giving,* which refers to sharing with others what one has of this world's goods; *Ruling,* which means, 'taking the lead,' which is the function of organizers, superintendents, and directors of Christian work; and *Mercy-showing,* which includes the care of the sick, the poor, the afflicted, and the sorrowing. This is the work of the visitor. No one can do all these things, but to each of us is given something to do; and Paul says that the gifts should be exercised with faith, with devotion, with diligence, with generosity, and with cheerfulness.

ROMANS 12,13

From the corporate responsibility of believers, Paul turns our attention to

Our Individual Responsibility (9-13)

In addition to the exercise of specific 'gifts,' there are certain qualities which all Christians should possess and exhibit for the benefit of fellow-believers. The root quality of all is named first,

> 'Let your love be unfeigned';

and then twelve ways are indicated in which this love will express itself.

The love spoken of is that of principle, not of sentiment; the 'love of God which is shed abroad in our hearts through the Holy Spirit.' The word has no epithet here, but stands in the magnificence of its own strength and simplicity. Only they who exhibit it have it; and they who claim to have it, yet do not exhibit it, are hypocrites.

To 'feign' is to hide what one is, and to pretend to be what one is not. Such a caricature smiles with one face, and frowns with another. A French writer has caustically said that 'hypocrisy is the homage which vice pays to virtue.' Paul says, 'let your love be real; not simulated, but sincere'; and when it is this, it will express itself in the manner indicated in the following twelve qualities.

The first quality is Moral Abhorrence: 'abhor that which is evil' (9). True love is not present where there is not a moral recoil from evil. In this day of spurious charity and unprincipled toleration, we should cultivate a healthy hatred of moral evil.

The second quality is Moral Adherence: 'cleave to that which is good' (9). This means that we should be glued

to the good.   Ideally evil will be abhorred in exact
proportion to one's adherence to good.   Let us
remember that these moral reactions are of the essence
of love.   Abhorring what is evil and cleaving to what
is good are inseparable qualities, and love in both
aspects is dynamic in society.

The third quality is *Family Affection:* '*In brotherly-love
be tenderly affectioned one to another*' (10).   There is a
love which we should have for all men, the love which
God has for all; but the '*affection*' here referred to is
limited to the members of the Christian family.   The
word *philadelphia* occurs in the New Testament seven
times, and always of love between Christians.   The
love of a blood-relationship necessarily differs from
every other, and in the Church it is by Christ's
blood.

The fourth quality is *Unselfish Deference:* '*In honour
preferring one another*' (10).   Or it might be rendered,
'outdo one another in showing honour.'   I suspect
that this is one of the most difficult exhortations, for
we all like to be honoured, and, maybe, we do not
exult when others are honoured and we are not.   He
who fulfils this exhortation is the embodiment of
Christian humility.

The fifth quality is *Unflagging Zeal:* '*In diligence not
slothful*' (11).   Luther translates this, '*Be not lazy as
to what you ought to do.*'   The exhortation implies
earnestness and thoroughness in the performance of
Christian duties.   Never let your zeal flag; keep up
the temperature of your spiritual life.

The sixth quality is *Vital Enthusiasm:* '*Be fervent
in spirit*' (11).   The word '*fervent*' means *to boil,* and
this is the positive side of the preceding negative;

not flagging, but boiling. It is by fire that water boils, and only by the flame of the Holy Spirit can our spirits reach this temperature.

The seventh quality is *Devout Service: 'Serving the Lord'* (11). There are half-a-dozen words translated *servant* in the New Testament. These signify a household servant, a healing servant, an attendant, ministry in any form, an under-rower, and the word used in our passage, a *bondslave,* which is the lowest in the scale of servitude. Paul never tired of calling himself Christ's *bondslave,* and fervently would he have sung

'My highest place is lying low at my Redeemer's feet;
No real joy in life I know, but in His service sweet.'

The eighth quality is *Joyful Hope: 'Rejoicing in hope'* (12); which means that our hope of coming glory, beginning with the Lord's Return, should keep us joyful, whatever our circumstances may be.

The ninth quality is *Patient Endurance: 'Patient in tribulation'* (12). Just because we have the hope of glory, we can, and should endure patiently the trials which will inevitably assail us. But for our hope it would not be possible to endure.

The tenth quality is *Persevering Prayerfulness: 'Continuing steadfastly in prayer'* (12). Prayer keeps all the other qualities in a state of health. It paints the rainbow of hope in the tears of tribulation. It puts the sunlight of heaven behind the darkest clouds, and makes them glorious with their exquisite tinting and drapery of purple and gold. Prayer shapes into beautiful and glorious forms the lava which the volcano of earthly disaster has sent forth in molten streams. Prayer is our best support in adversity, and our best protection in prosperity. He does not live who does not pray.

The eleventh quality is *Practical Generosity: 'Distributing to the necessities of saints'* (13). After private blessing comes public benevolence. First, devotion to God, and then, helpfulness to men. The true order is to reach man by God, not to reach God by man. The heart is first drawn out, and then the purse. Pious verbiage can never compensate for the want of practical sympathy. Said a visitor to a person in urgent temporal need: 'Never mind, you'll get a crown one day'; and the needy soul replied, 'but I wouldna mind half-a-crown now, to be going on with.'

The twelfth quality is *Watchful Hospitality: 'Pursuing hospitality'* (13). It is not easy in these days to keep 'open house,' and generally it is impossible; but, in these austere times, the spirit of hospitality must not be allowed to perish.

> Is thy cruse of comfort failing?
>   Rise and share it with a friend;
> And through all the years of famine,
>   It shall serve thee to the end.
>
> For the heart grows rich in giving;
>   All its wealth is living grain;
> Seeds which mildew in the garner,
>   Scattered, fill with gold the plain.

These, then, are the qualities which each of us is exhorted to exhibit toward our fellow-believers, and it is a programme of graces which will keep us busy for some time to come.

Having considered our duty to the Church (4-13), the Apostle now calls attention to

2.   OUR DUTY TO THE WORLD (12:14-21)

He names eleven things which should characterize the Christian's attitude toward the world, and these, which cover much ground, may well cause us reproachful reflection.   Let us look rapidly at these exhortations.

1. BENEFICENCE: '*Bless those who pursue you; bless and do not curse*' (14).

In the previous verse we are told to '*pursue*' hospitality and here we are told that the enemy will '*pursue*' us. Persecution may take an infinite variety of forms, but in all, our attitude toward the persecutor is to be one, not of imprecation, but of intercession.   Paul derived this exhortation from his Master Who said: 'Bless those who curse you, and pray for those who despitefully use you' (Luke vi. 28).   This will not be easy, but it will be right.

2. SYMPATHY.   '*Rejoice with the rejoicing, and weep with the weeping*' (15).

There are times when we can and should congratulate people who are not Christians; and certainly there are times when we should condole with them. If we show pleasure at a birth, and sorrow at a death, we have done something towards securing their interest in spiritual things.

3. HARMONY: '*Keep in harmony with one another*' (16).

There are many things of a human kind which give us opportunity for friendliness with non-Christians; matters relating to recreation, reading, daily happenings, and much more about which we can talk and in which we can engage; and to show that we have much in common, may lead others towards the things that matter most.   We must find points of contact with those whom we would win. Jesus' point of contact with the Samaritan woman was the water in the well.

4. HUMILITY: *'Aspire not to pre-eminence, but associate with the lowly'* (16).

The 'lofty' must be interpreted in the light of the 'lowly.' The exhortation is not against every form of ambition, but against seeking pre-eminence for oneself. Let us remember that humanity's high things are often divinity's low things. A corrective to unholy ambition is association with the lowly, and remember, the lowly are not the low. The exhortation may mean, 'associate with lowly folk'; or, 'give yourself to lowly tasks'; in either case it is humility on the part of the Christian which is enjoined.

5. SELF-COMPLACENCY: *'Be not wise according to your own judgment'* (16).

The Christian must not behave in such a way as to draw the just criticism of unbelievers; and certainly he does this when he is conceited. Conceit is vanity, and generally is exhibited by those who have least reason so to pose. Corn, when it is green, is upright, but when it is ripe it bends low. A vain young man was a great trial to Mr. Moody, and one day he said to the evangelist, 'You know, Mr. Moody, I am a self-made man'; to which Mr. Moody replied, 'Young man, you have relieved the Almighty of a great responsibility.' (This reply is attributed also to Earl Lloyd George!) People like that succeed only in making themselves ridiculous.

6. RETALIATION: *'Requite to no man wrong for wrong'* (17).

It is no business of a Christian to try to 'get even'

ROMANS 12,13

with someone who has done him an injustice. Two blacks do not make a white. Hitting back is not a virtue, but a vice. It is human to retaliate, but it is divine not to do so. When 'Old Adam' rises to strike we've got to say, 'sit down; you're dead.' When Jesus was reviled, He reviled not again; and when He suffered, He threatened not, but committed Himself to Him that judgeth righteously.

7. GOODNESS: *'Be absorbed in what is good for all men to see'* (17).

The world is the Christian's most acute, and, perhaps, most accurate critic. Christianity is held in high regard by most people, and it is when Christians act inconsistently with it that we hear the world's criticism. People recognize goodness when they see it, and it is goodness we are to provide in the sight of everyone. Our conduct should be above suspicion, and should have in it the quality which is called *goodness*. Of the many tributes paid to the late King, one, oft repeated, is that 'he was a good man.' To be *correct* in our conduct is not enough; we should be *attractive* also. Our tree should not only bear fruit, but also cultivate leaves.

8. PEACEABLENESS: *'If it be possible, so far as it depends on you, be at peace with all men'* (18).

Paul does not say that peace will always be possible, but he does say, 'let the want of it not be due to *you*'. We are answerable only for our part in our relations with others. Peace is always to be devoutly sought, but not at any price. Strife upsets the nerves, disturbs the mind, and arrests spiritual progress. 'As far as it depends on you' implies that a point may be reached at which principle must take precedence of peace.

Dispeace with anyone should never be due on our part to pique, but to principle. There is, of course, the peace of a cemetery, but that is not what is enjoined here.

9. NON-AVENGEMENT: '*Avenge not yourselves, beloved, but give place unto wrath*' (19).

Three meanings have been given to this reference to '*wrath*'; one, that the Christian is to restrain his own wrath; another, that he is to yield to the anger of his opponent; and a third, that the wrath is God's, and that just because He will deal with His and His people's enemies, the Christian should not. As God alone knows all the facts, and as His actions are free from vindictiveness, we should leave the judging of evildoers to Him.

10. MAGNANIMITY: '*Give your enemy food and drink*' (20).

This is the Christian's form of revenge, and is the antithesis of retaliation. The reference embraces all sorts of kindness, and implies that in this way hostility may be broken down, and the enemy brought to repentance.

The last reference in this section is to

11. CONQUEST: '*Be not conquered by evil; but conquer evil with good*' (21).

Our attitude towards wrongs done to us will determine whether we conquer evil, or whether we are conquered by it. If we show the same spirit as the enemy, he has conquered; but if we act as Christians should, he is conquered. This principle is of wide application, and is one of the secrets of Christian conquest. If I had the opportunity to live my life over again, some things I have done, I would not do; some things I have said, would remain unuttered

ROMANS 12,13

and some letters I have written, would never be penned. This Epistle says that we can be 'more than conquerors', and as we *can* be, we *should* be, so let us resolve that 'though Him Who loved us,' we *will* be.

But our obligations are not yet exhausted. We have been thinking of them in relation to the *Church*, and to the *World*, and now, briefly, we must consider

3. OUR DUTY TO THE STATE (13:1-7)

This is the only passage in which Paul deals with this subject in detail; (a similar passage is in 1 Peter ii. 13-17). Though briefly treated the importance of the subject is great, and its scope and limits are defined and illustrated in many places in both Testaments.

In these seven verses at least seven things are said: (1) that we should be subject to the State because it is a Divine Institution; (2) that resistance to constituted authority is resistance to God, and will be punished; (3) that rulers, viewed ideally, are God's ministers, appointed to encourage what is good, and to punish what is evil; (4) that only evil-doers have anything to fear from properly constituted authority; (5) that we should be subject to the State not only from fear of the consequences of disobedience, but because it is right to obey; (6) that the matter of taxation is an illustration of the ruler's power to impose, and of our obligation to submit; and (7) that we should fulfil our manifold obligations to the State.

This passage does not deal with the *whole* problem of a Christian's relation to the State, and if we look to it for guidance on aspects of the subject to which it does not refer, we shall be disappointed. But even relative to what *is* said, much is left to legitimate inference.

State government is viewed *ideally*, and not as too often it *actually* is; and no form of government is prescribed, Monarchical, Republican, or any other. What is insisted on is that State government is of God, and that all who are under it should respect it. Because Christians have a citizenship in heaven, they are not absolved from their citizenship on earth, nor from its obligations.

This passage has nothing to say about political parties, nor, except implicitly, to voting; but relative to the latter, surely Christians should use their influence to secure good rulers, and to exclude bad ones! In an organized community taxes are necessarily imposed, and Christians must pay them, though we cannot now get them out of the mouths of fish. By the State we are protected against the ravages of anarchy, and all privileges carry with them obligations.

It has been well said that 'the fact that an earthly government may be corrupt and tyrannical does not disprove the Divine origin of government, any more than the fact that parents may be unfaithful to their duties proves that the family is not divinely originated, or the fact that a particular church may become corrupt proves that the Church is not Divine in its source' (Shedd).

But what is here said does not imply that the Christian must never, in any circumstances, disobey constituted authority. Our first allegiance is to God, and if the State requires of us what would violate our loyalty to God, then we must resist. When Nebuchadnezzar commanded the three Hebrews to worship

ROMANS 12,13

his image, they refused; and when Darius prohibited prayer to anyone but himself, Daniel disobeyed; and when Christians were ordered to worship Cæsar, they would not, and were thrown to the lions.

Christ has said the last word on this subject: 'Render to Cæsar the things that are Cæsar's, and to God, the things that are God's.'

Here, then, are detailed our duty to the Church (xii. 4-13); to the World (xii. 14-21); and to the State (xiii. 1-7); our religious, and social, and civil duties; and inevitably we ask, 'how can we fulfil these duties?' The Apostle answers this question by revealing

(ii) The Impelling Power of the Christian Life (13:8-10)

'Owe no man anything but to love one another.'

Debts are dishonourable. They show, either that one has incurred a liability which he cannot meet, or else, being able to pay, he is unwilling to do so. Either way the debt is disgraceful. There must be many professing the name of Christ who are guilty of debt. They pray, but they do not pay; and failure to do the latter renders worthless their diligence in the former. Debt is a form of stealing, for it is keeping for oneself something which belongs to someone else. Some honest people are brought into debt because others will not pay to them what they owe, and such are entitled to sympathy. We must be careful not to regard as sinful a reasonable delay in the payment of an account, but our passage refers to debts that can and should be avoided. I would rather be a suffering creditor than a shameful debtor. Perhaps some of you will have to pay today.

But there are debts other than monetary. We can owe people coin of other mints. Do we not owe to others forgiveness, and patience, and sympathy, and appreciation, and gratitude, and generosity? Have you paid in the coin of gratitude the debt you owe to the person who led you to Christ? It may be that you have not even troubled to write a letter to him, or her, and express thanks for that eternal service.

Are you getting spiritual help from your minister? If so, have you ever said so to him; or do you write to him only when you have something to criticize? Then, is there not another debt which we have not paid, or only partly so, the debt of prayers for others. Think of all who need your prayers, and then say if you have paid this debt.

Last year, for a long time, I was very ill, and many of you prayed for me, and I want to thank you now. You prayed for me when I could not pray for myself, and God heard you, and answered. I thank you.

But there is a debt we can never fully discharge, and that is to 'love one another.' This debt we must be forever paying, yet never clearing. The more of it that is paid, the more is felt to be due. We owe it to all men to tell them what we know about the love of Christ. The love enjoined cannot be an outward rule of life unless it is first an inward principle. True love never asks, 'how much must I give?' but, 'how much can I give?' If we all loved as we should, we would never owe any other debt; and love alone would enable us to fulfil our duty to the Church, to the World, and to the State.

But the Apostle has one more thing to say relative

to what he has said in these two chapters, and this relates to

(iii) THE GREAT INCENTIVE to the Christian Life (13:11-14)

This incentive is the Second Advent of Christ.

'Now is our salvation nearer to us than when we first believed. The night is far spent, and the day is at hand.'

In this weighty passage, past, future, and present are brought together. *Past:* 'the night is far spent'; *future:* 'the day is at hand'; and *present: 'let us* cast off the works of darkness'; *'let us* put on the armour of light'; and *'let us* walk decently as in the day.' And why all this? Because final 'salvation is nearer to us than when we first believed'; or, in other words, because *Christ is coming.* The Christians of the Apostolic age believed that He would come in their time; and about that, let it be said, that whereas their *perspective* was wrong, their *hope* was right. Alas, that for long centuries since then, both the perspective and the hope of multitudes of Christians have been wrong. Early the truth about the Lord's Return faded from view, and the Church set out to save the world. It has had over a millennium and a half in which to do so, and today the world is further from being saved than ever it has been.

What, then, is the present duty? Paul says it is threefold. First, 'WAKE UP.' All the Virgins 'slumbered and slept,' and through these centuries, notwithstanding endless religious, social and intellectual activities, the Church which has not known, or has denied, that the Lord is coming-again, has been asleep; and the call rings out in this fateful hour of history, '*Wake up—wake up—wake up!*'

And having wakened up, our second duty is to DRESS PROPERLY. There are clothes to be '*cast off*,' and clothes to be '*put on.*' Our night vestments, called '*the works of the darkness*,' are to be cast aside, and in their place we are to '*put on the weapons of the light.*' We cannot put on the *weapons* on top of the *works*, any more than we can put our clothes on in the morning on top of our pyjamas. In the place of '*works*' must come *war*, for '*weapons*' are for defence and holy aggression; for when we realize that Christ is coming, and may-be soon, we shall stop building castles, and get into the conflict.

The third thing Paul says we must do is to ACT RIGHTLY; we are to '*walk decently*,' as becomes people whose daily strength is in the conviction that their Lord is on the way, and that at any time they may see 'the flaming of His advent feet.'

> In the fading of the starlight
> We can see the coming morn;
> And the lights of men are paling
> In the splendours of the dawn;
> For the eastern skies are glowing
> As with lights of hidden fire,
> And the hearts of men are stirring
> With the throb of deep desire.

For the Christian the best is yet to be. We are facing, not the night, but the morning. Danger is departing, and deliverance is dawning. So let us rejoice.

Having pointed out our Paths of Duty, the Apostle, in a final portion, calls our attention to certain Principles of Action.

ROMANS 12,13

4

PRINCIPLES OF ACTION
(Romans 14:1-15:13)

I MUCH regret that want of time does not allow of a careful, detailed exposition of this very important passage. All that can be attempted now is to discern the main features of the argument.

Paul has said: 'Owe no man anything but to love one another,' and now he applies that principle to a particular case.

The parties referred to are '*the weak*,' and '*the strong*.' 'The weak' are those whose conduct is regulated by certain *scruples* which they hold; and 'the strong' are those who act on the principle of Christian *liberty*; and in both cases the matters under consideration are without moral significance, matters relative to *food*, and the observance of *days*.

In discussing this matter the Apostle speaks very frankly to both parties; and the substance of what he says is: first, *you should exhibit mutual toleration* (xiv. 1-12); secondly, *you should recognize brotherly obligation* (xiv. 13-23); and thirdly, *you should act with Christlike consideration* (xv. 1-13); and these requirements are as applicable now as they were then, and to more things than 'food,' and 'days.'

MUTUAL TOLERATION (14:1-12)

Paul will not let us get away from the present by the contemplation of the future. He has just been pointing us to a wonderful day which certainly will dawn. Lest, however, we fold our hands, and abandon ourselves to the horizon, he continues: 'But him that is weak in the faith receive ye, yet, not to discuss his doubts.' Heaven is related to earth; the future to the present; the divine to the human; and, our hope to our duty. Spirituality does not consist in dreaming, but in doing. We all, at times, are disposed to sing, 'O for the wings, for the wings of a dove; then would I fly away and be at rest.' But how do you know you would not light upon a thorn! Rest is not found by flying away, but by filling our days with duties well done.

It can be said of the 'weak' of whom Paul speaks, what Christ said of the poor, 'they are ever with us'; but the 'strong' must be careful what they think and say about them, and how they act towards them. It is easy to say, 'Oh, these are cranks, leave them alone'; but that gets no one anywhere. It is best to face the fact that there are Christians with scruples, and to respect them, when we cannot follow them.

The matter of diet even now is not a dead issue; and relative to it the 'strong' brother is in danger of despising the 'weak'; and the 'weak' brother is in danger of judging the 'strong.'

A invites *B* to dinner and puts before him a good joint of pork. He invites *B* to ask a blessing, and *B* says:

> 'O Lord, if Thou canst bless in this dispensation
> what Thou didst curse in the last, bless this pig.'

But *B* will not have any of the pig. *A* smiles contemptuously, and *B* hurls at him Leviticus xi. 7, 'And the swine, he is unclean to you'; and judges *A*'s

loyalty to the Word of God.   *A* tells *B* to read 1 Timothy
iv. 4, 5, 'Every creature of God is good, and nothing
to be refused, if it be received with thanksgiving;
for it is sanctified by the Word of God and prayer';
and there follows an argument, which is well spiced
with recriminations.

Meanwhile the pork gets cold; the cook is annoyed;
the brethren are rattled; each sticks to his point
instead of to his joint; fellowship is broken; and *A*
does not invite *B* to dinner again.

How pathetic and tragic! and all over a bit of pork
for which *A* thanks God, as well he may, if he can get
it.

Now, both these men are wrong in spirit; the one
for *despising*, and the other for *judging*, though both
are right in what they do conscientiously.   Then
why not be tolerant in things indifferent!   *A* should
eat his pork, and *B* his vegetables, and they should
have a happy time together 'in the Lord.'

And as for the observance of days—I remember
the time when, in the Highlands of Scotland, the
blinds were pulled down on Sundays and the pianos
were locked, and no one was allowed to go for a walk.
And there are many people to-day who think it
wrong to go to Church in any way other than on foot;
but where they go astray is in thinking that those
who do employ mechanical transport are breaking a
divine law, and are guilty.

Let us remember that 'we shall all stand before the
Judgment-seat of Christ,' and 'each one of us shall
give account of himself to God' (10, 12); and then,
Henry will not accuse Thomas of eating only vegetables, nor James accuse Robert of eating animal

flesh, nor Mary accuse Ellen of going about without
a hat, nor Ethel accuse Amy of not being an Episco-
palian, nor Keble accuse Kelly of not having observed
'The Christian Year.'

What will matter then is whether we truly loved
the Lord; whether we were diligent in His service;
whether we sought to win souls; whether we were
tolerant and forgiving among ourselves; whether we
loved our Bibles, and delighted in prayer; whether
we were filled with the Holy Spirit; and because
these things will matter *then*, they matter *now*.

Then let the 'weak' brother not be censorious; and
let the 'strong' brother not be contemptuous. We've
got to learn to be tolerant in matters indifferent.

BROTHERLY OBLIGATION (14:13-23)

The Apostle, who in verses 1-12 has been addressing
both the 'weak' and 'strong' brothers, now addresses
more especially the 'strong,' and his design is to show
that there is something greater than *Christian liberty*,
and this is *Christian love*.

It is not always right for us to do all that it would
be right for us to do! The 'weak' cannot win the
'strong' to the level of weakness; but the 'strong' may
be able to win the 'weak' to the level of strength;
but this will not be done by the 'strong' insisting
always on his liberty. All things lawful for us are not
always expedient. If by exercising our liberty we
injure the spiritual life of a believer whose light is
limited, we do violence to the law of love, which is
the highest known principle of action. Each of us
is exercising a definite influence on others every day.
Scientists tell us that every time we raise our arm

ROMANS 14:1-15:13

or lift our foot, or sit down or rise up, we affect the balance of the whole universe, yet we are not conscious of so doing. Likewise, in the moral realm, every word we speak, and our every deed, as well as the things we say not, and do not, are affecting people far and wide, and this influence is, for the most part, unconscious. Remember this in the shop, and hospital, and factory, and barracks, and camp, and club, and home.

It is quite possible to injure a fellow-believer by actions lawful in themselves, and by insisting on rights which God has given to us. Because Christ *died* to save us all, we should be willing to sacrifice some rights to prevent a brother from going wrong.

What the strong brother does is not wrong in itself (16), but if he insists on it at the cost of the weak brother's enlightenment and advancement, he takes a heavy and solemn responsibility (15). The material and the spiritual, the temporal and the eternal, are never commensurate, and to insist on the former at the expense of the latter, is not only to see things out of perspective, but is also a deplorable evidence of selfishness.

In actual practice it may be difficult to decide how far one should go in the way of self-denial in concession to the scruples of those who are weak in the faith (1), but the principle is here plainly set forth.

And now, finally,

CHRISTLIKE CONSIDERATION (15:1-13)

The Apostle has one more thing to say on the subject of brothers weak and strong, and then his Epistle will end, except for some concluding personal matters. And what he has to say is, that in this, as indeed in all things, _Christ's example is our standard._

> 'We that are able ought to bear the weaknesses
> of the unable, and not to _please_ ourselves. Let each
> of us _please_ his neighbour, as regards what is good,
> with a view to edification. For even Christ did
> not _please_ Himself' (1-3).

You will observe that the word '_please_' occurs three times here, and it means, not a servile and compromising deference to human opinion, not the complaisance of the parasite who fawns and flatters, but 'the unselfish and watchful aim to meet half-way, if possible, the thought and feeling of a fellow-disciple' (Moule). In this sense it means to gratify, and so to satisfy. _Pleasing_ differs from _obeying_, in that the latter is a _duty_, whereas the former is a _privilege. Pleasing_ is _obedience_ with a _plus._ You tell your child to do his homework before you return in the evening, and when you arrive you find that he has _obeyed;_ but he has done more than that, he has put your slippers by the fire to warm, for the night is cold, and he did it to _please_ you. In like manner to _please_ God is more than to _obey_ Him; and when we sacrifice some liberty which is ours in order to be helpful to a neighbour, we are pleasing both God and him, and are following Christ's example, 'Who did not please Himself.' And on that note we conclude our studies.

How amazing a revelation has been set before us. We have been shown the way from _Condemnation_ to _Glory_ by _Justification_ and _Sanctification,_ and then we have been told, while still short of Glory, how we should behave in the _Church,_ in the _World,_ and in the _State;_ and how we should use any enlightenment we

ROMANS 14:1-15:13

have for the benefit of those not so well enlightened. In all this the highest doctrines are related to the humblest duties, and it is made plain *what it means to be a true Christian*.

> 'And now unto Him that is able to do exceeding abundantly above all that we ask or think, according to the power that worketh in us, unto Him be glory in the Church, and in Christ Jesus, unto all generations, for ever and ever,   Amen.'